Praise For

Retooling America's Educational System

"Ready to learn about the tragic failure of the American education system? Forget the daily media onslaught about what's wrong with American education and read Gordon Love's *Retooling America's Educational System*, to find the truth.

Love proposes a Y-track system, with one road leading to a college education, and the other leading to vocational programs resulting in apprenticeship programs for hands-on careers in the building and construction trades, manufacturing, and forgotten-but-lucrative services like auto technician and truck driver.

Retooling uses relevant data from reliable sources like the US Census Bureau and the Bureau of Labor Statistics. Data can be difficult to interpret when presented in academic jargon, but not here.

Read this book to recognize fact from political and media fiction. The American education system needs to be retooled, and Gordon Love tells us how to accomplish this in his masterpiece."

—John Henry Weiss, former teacher and author of
HIRED! FIRED! RETIRED! Navigating Your Career in the Worldwide Workplace

Retooling America's Educational System:
Removing the Stigmas and Discriminatory Practices Against
Career Technical Education

by Gordon L. Love

© Copyright 2025 Gordon L. Love

979-8-88824-791-4

All rights reserved. No part of this publication may be reproduced, stored in a retrieval system, or transmitted in any form or by any means—electronic, mechanical, photocopy, recording, or any other—except for brief quotations in printed reviews, without the prior written permission of the author.

Published by

◂köehlerbooks™

3705 Shore Drive
Virginia Beach, VA 23455
800-435-4811
www.koehlerbooks.com

RETOOLING AMERICA'S EDUCATIONAL SYSTEM

**REMOVING THE STIGMAS
AND DISCRIMINATORY PRACTICES
AGAINST CAREER TECHNICAL EDUCATION**

GORDON L. LOVE

VIRGINIA BEACH
CAPE CHARLES

TABLE OF CONTENTS

CHAPTER ONE
    The Current Status of Education in America 1
CHAPTER TWO
    Improving Education and
    Training Systems in the US 12
CHAPTER THREE
    Is the Educational Environment
    Open or Closed? 27
CHAPTER FOUR
    Developing Partnerships Between
    Business, Industry, and Education 33
CHAPTER FIVE
    Union vs. Nonunion Workforces
    and the Impact of Right-to-Work Legislation
    on the Current Apprenticeship System 38
CHAPTER SIX
    Once Upon a Time in Our Educational System
    — How Close We Were to the Perfect
    Dual-Track Delivery System 44
CHAPTER SEVEN
    The Apprenticeship-Development Program 51
CHAPTER EIGHT
    Introduction to the American
    Apprenticeship System 58
CHAPTER NINE
    In Conclusion:
    Implementing the Y-Track System of Education 71

BIBLIOGRAPHY 79

CHAPTER ONE

The Current Status of Education in America

America is often called the greatest country in the world, yet our educational and training systems are falling behind other countries. The Program for International Student Assessment (PISA) delivers testing to assess the performance of fifteen-year-olds in reading, math, and science. In their reports from 2022, the students from the US scored in the average range in comparison to eighty other countries.[1] We are also failing to produce the needed human resources for a vibrant labor force. On July 31, 2022, the Bureau of Labor Statistics reported a shortage of 6.3 million workers and 11.2 million unfilled jobs.[2]

Our American society has consistently improved in the fight against discrimination and has developed antidiscrimination laws in the areas of race, sexual orientation, gender, disability, etc. In the educational realm, we have implemented specialized accommodation services for disabled students and discrimination-awareness training for teachers and educational staff. For example, students requiring special-education services receive an Individualized Education Program (IEP), which articulates the special-education instruction,

---

1   "PISA 2022 U.S. Results," National Center for Education Statistics, https://nces.ed.gov/surveys/pisa/pisa2022/index.asp
2   Arthak Adhikari and Tamara Mickle, "What Is the Unemployed People Per Job Openings Ratio? A 21-Year Case Study into Unemployment Trends," Beyond the Numbers 11, no. 6 (U.S. Bureau of Labor Statistics, 2022), https://www.bls.gov/opub/btn/volume-11/what-is-the-unemployed-people-per-job-openings-ratio-a-21-year-case-study-into-unemployment-trends.htm.

support, and services a student needs to thrive in school. Working with and accommodating the different learning styles of students is encouraged, and teachers are trained on preventing discrimination based on sexual orientation. Unfortunately, more improvement is still needed. America's current education system unknowingly discriminates against nearly half of our student population.

Students are routinely coached to pursue a college education, and, often, few other options are discussed. Pupils are directed into two separate "boxes" at an early age, and as they progress through the system, this guidance becomes more consistent. Box #1 contains the students who are on a college-bound track. Of the 2.7 million high schoolers who graduated in the first nine months of 2021, some 1.7 million (or 62 percent) were enrolled in college in October 2021.[3] Box #2 is a general-education track and contains the rest of the students. Students in this box, a non-college-bound track, comprise 38 percent of the high school graduates, many of whom are left to flounder without a career path or plan after high school graduation.

For students choosing the college-bound track, how many graduate with a degree from college? The National Center for Education Statistics reveals that in 2020, the overall six-year graduation rate for first-time, full-time undergraduate students who began seeking bachelor's degrees at four-year degree-granting institutions in fall 2014 was 64 percent.[4] This means that out of all high school graduates, around 60 percent don't end up earning a college degree. So what happens to this majority? Are they left to flounder without a career path?

Unfortunately, students have been led to believe that a career in manufacturing or in the trades—as a construction worker, electrician, plumber, automotive technician, etc.—is less prestigious than going

---

3 "Immediate College Enrollment Rate," Condition of Education, National Center for Education Statistics, last updated May 2024, https://nces.ed.gov/programs/coe/indicator/cpa.

4 "Undergraduate Retention and Graduation Rates," Condition of Education, National Center for Education Statistics, last updated May 2022, https://nces.ed.gov/programs/coe/indicator/ctr.

to college. In addition, they often think they won't make as much money as those with college degrees. These misguided students often don't complete their college education or obtain a degree that has very limited value, which may cause them to accrue college loan debt and possibly return home to live with their parents. Many of these students pick up part-time work and shift from one job to the next. The lucky ones might connect with a job in manufacturing or a sector that offers apprenticeship training, eventually getting hired for a position that will support a family and allow them to participate in the middle class.

This is why our educational system must be upgraded for the purpose of maximizing our human resources. We need to stop wasting time, money, and human resources when many of these students could have been placed into a career technical path that leads into a tech prep program or an apprenticeship certificate.

Because of the success that we had in the early 1990s until 2005 in career and technical education, which I'll outline later, I have been passionate about bringing this information forward so that it may be a resource for several of the new school-to-apprenticeship sites that are being piloted across the country today. In this book, I will recommend a plan that would meet the needs for academic improvement and a vibrant American workforce through the implementation of a dual-track, what I call a "Y-track" educational system. I am including a step-by-step process and how-to instructions for implementing career-development systems, career and technical education programs (CTE), and apprenticeships in K–12 education and into college.

The existing American apprenticeship remains today as one of the most viable training systems. A major key player in this step is the involvement of community colleges who offer the related training components and the successful implementation of education "bridges" without duplication between K–12 and community colleges. Also included are explanations of the related factors that are keeping the US from moving forward, such as the decline of the unions in our workforce and the "right-to-work" state legislation issues and the impact this has on the American training system.

During the last fifteen years that I've worked in CTE there has been a decline in US manufacturing. A shift has occurred from manufacturing to a more service-oriented economy. In the CTE institution where I was employed, an overall drop in student enrollment resulted in the closing of the welding program and later the closing of the plastics program. This trend has continued, and we now have a shortage of qualified workers in trade and technical areas.

Although great strides have been made in establishing more funding for CTE, there continues to be a large gap in funding between the forgotten half of our students who often can't afford to go to college and the 62 percent who do go on to college (though, as we discussed, not all of that 62 percent actually earns their degree anyway).

The Smith–Hughes Act of 1917 was the first authorization for federal vocation-education funding. Subsequent legislation for vocational education (now termed career and technical education) included the Vocational Act of 1973 and the Carl D. Perkins Act of 1984. Perkins was reauthorized in 1990 (Perkins II) and 1998 (Perkins III). In 2006, significant bipartisan legislation was enacted with Perkins IV. It has been a principal source of federal funding and discretionary grants for the purpose of improving secondary and postsecondary CTE programs in the US. The most recent reauthorization of the Perkins Act was in 2018 (Perkins V). It has extensively amended Perkins IV through the Strengthening Career and Technical Education for the 21st Century Act.[5] This expanded investment in the reauthorized Perkins Act will help more Americans obtain relevant skills and high-paying jobs, while at the same time minimizing the costs of postsecondary education to students and their families. It encourages the expansion of apprenticeships that provide paid, relevant workplace experiences and opportunities as

---

5 "Perkins V," Legislation and Regulations, Perkins Collaborative Resource Network, effective May 2025, https://cte.ed.gov/legislation/perkins-v.

part of multiple pathways that begin earlier in a student's education, preferably in high school.

Successfully restructuring our current educational system must be a shared effort between educators, families, communities, businesses, and the government. Many are beginning to realize that something is wrong with our system as it exists currently. This is why people are breaking away from traditional state-run schools and turning to private schools, homeschooling, charter schools, and schools of choice. Imagine how great our educational system would be if involved parents no longer felt the need to pull their children out of state-run organizations to place them in charter or private schools, feeling instead like they have a voice within their local public schools. Administration and school boards must become more transparent and actively listen to parents to allow an exchange of information and dialogue. This can be achieved!

In addition, our local businesses have so much to offer our educational processes but are often shut out by our schools because they fear losing control of the educational process. Unions are also being run out of many organizations, yet they have been a critical foundation for the training and education of many of our young adults pursuing technical careers. I have seen firsthand that excellence in education can be achieved in a proper educational structure with the support of parents, educators, communities, and businesses. When local businesses become partners in education, innovative learning experiences can be provided. These are the ingredients of a successful educational system.

My background is in career and technical education and business in the states of Michigan and Wyoming. Working in my father's construction business allowed me the opportunity to become a trained carpenter and later a building contractor. Early on in my career I wanted to continue to play college football and went on to receive my undergraduate degree in industrial education. I have held various teaching positions at the high school and community college levels, taught at the Hines VA Hospital as a blind-rehabilitation instructor, and served as both a high school wrestling and football coach. I have a master's degree in CTE and educational leadership, and I worked as a career-placement coordinator for fifteen years, eventually becoming a certified Global Career Development Facilitator. It was at this time that I began working with the apprenticeship system and its relationship to education, business, and industry.

In the 1980s, I was hired by the Kent Intermediate School District in Michigan and worked at the Kent Career Technical Center. I was initially employed as a building-trades instructor and then transitioned to becoming their work-based learning coordinator. I was also designated as the first School-to-Registered Apprenticeship (STRA) coordinator in Michigan, where I began implementing a full career-education process for the K–12 student population.

The task I was assigned to was to develop work-based learning activities for the students at a career technical center and develop a placement office that was responsive to student outcomes in seeking a career. I was part of a team responsible for implementing the "Applied-Technology Curriculum Model," brainstormed and initiated by our director. This model had four components: career education, technology education, work-based learning, and applied academics. It was an exciting time in education. I was involved in many committees with educators as well as business and industry personnel. I received extensive training across the country in various curriculum models and strategies involving discipline, diversity, student assessment, career development, principles of management, and school improvement. New, exciting strategies emerged to promote student achievement and improve the school climate. We hosted several educational workshops and implemented many of these new strategies, while helping our local educators with strategies that worked specifically for their populations. This process was instrumental in testing some of these approaches and helped us to finalize a list of best practices. I eventually became the president of the Michigan Career Placement Association and gave presentations and training around the state on developing and implementing apprenticeships and career-development programs.

One of my many teaching assignments was with a group of high school students in inner-city high schools, primarily with alternative education students. Many of these students were expelled from traditional schools for poor grades, problems with attendance, or behavioral issues. This experience reinforced how parental/family/mentor support helps promote positive learning experiences for students, as well as how disastrous the consequences can be for those that do not have a supportive home life or positive mentor. I had students from rival city gangs in one of my classrooms, which added another interesting and tense set of dynamics. The goal was to bring these students back into the mainstream of society by giving them the skills they could use in the real world, shaping them into responsible citizens.

Throughout the class, we taught students how to build a house, training them to function professionally in a job and giving them necessary life skills in the process. Respect, discipline, structure, teamwork, technical skills, and applied academics—as well as a sense of pride in a job well done—were key training components for these students. Sadly, a couple of these students eventually lost their lives in street-gang shootings, but many of them turned their lives around and were also awarded scholarships to go on with their education and training. This was one of the most challenging positions that I've ever held, but it also became one of the most rewarding. To witness these young people alter the trajectory of their lives by learning, achieving, working as a team, and respecting others was inspiring. I'm still in contact with some of these former students now that they are adults, and they have become productive members of society, boasting the necessary skills to support their families and grateful that they were given the opportunity.

During my years spent in education, I have worked with some amazing educators that love their jobs and take their students' education very seriously. I have seen teachers sacrifice and use their own money to purchase supplies and even prescription glasses for their students. One teacher in our CTE center donated one of her kidneys to a student for transplant. These selfless, compassionate, excellent teachers are key to student learning. I have collaborated with numerous educational administrators, including academic principals, CTE directors, assistant principals, assistant directors, and superintendents over the years, and they make a tremendous difference in the outcome of the students. Strong leaders that follow consistent standards in dealing with staff, students, and parents can shape the learning climate in a school. Of course, there are still a small number of teachers and administrators that desperately need help to improve their educational strategies; however, this is the minority.

A vision for bringing technical help to employers all over Michigan was established in the early 1970s by building a series of vocational training centers around the state. Many of these career centers originated through the funding of the Vocational Education Act of 1963 and were later reauthorized by the Carl D. Perkins Act of 1984. These centers would educate high school juniors and seniors in a variety of technical trades, which included everything from building, welding, manufacturing, agriscience, automotive repair, architectural design, culinary arts, health careers, and many more. Many experts in technology fields sat on educational advisory committees to give industry input and test students for competency once they completed a program.

The CTE center that I worked for had a compensation system based on merit. The educators would receive a base salary, and when the advisory-committee members tested students at the end of each semester, the instructors would receive additional pay based on student success, including their knowledge and skill performance. (Talk about accountability!) Often teachers were stressed about having part of their pay based on student performance, but I believe this was an excellent way to guarantee that students achieved their full potential.

Although this system was later changed to a more traditional pay system in order to run in sync with traditional academic education, I would like to see a merit-based pay system reinstituted into CTE because it played a great role in the success of students' training.

One of the guidelines that was established during my time in Michigan was in the administrative-management requirements of vocational-education training systems. To be a principal or administrative director in one of the CTE facilities, it was recommended that leaders have a vocational background and be vocationally authorized to be part of the management team. In recent years, the school boards and superintendents have allowed nonvocational people to take leadership roles, and it has radically changed the complexion of these facilities. In fact, some of the vocational-technical centers of today hardly resemble what the original charter guidelines had intended. Many of the technical programs have either been eliminated or downsized to the point that they are hardly recognizable.

Some CTE schools have changed so radically that they more closely resemble a typical academic school than a career technical center. Administrators refer to this type of center as a "school within a school," and they still fall under the local charter guidelines as set forth by the state. These centers, once thriving CTE schools, become smothered by academia, and in turn, their technical programs get watered down.

The purpose of these programs originally was to offer educational and career opportunities to students and feed the local industry with human resources. But currently, they are falling short of that goal. CTE centers have dropped many of their technical programs because of the declining economy, with many companies moving south and abroad to get cheaper labor and reduce their taxes. The short-term need for skilled workers began to drop off after 2005, and management teams assumed that programs needed to be reduced, despite the national data on employee shortages that had been predicted for years. This trend, along with the mass retiring of baby boomers, has been going on for the last fifteen to twenty years and has now caused a serious shortage in technically trained people with the skills needed to fill the employment gap. With the unemployment of our nontechnically trained citizens hovering at record highs, the need to produce highly skilled workers is paramount.

Companies in the manufacturing sector are now faced with a real shortage of technical help and are floundering to find an adequate number of skilled employees. As such, some companies resort to recruiting foreign labor. With this internal collapse occurring, our CTE centers are allowing a large share of the equipment to be auctioned off, and rebuilding these programs with proper equipment and safety measures will be costly.

Over the past century, our society has slowly transformed itself from an industrial giant into the more service-oriented economy of today. In fact, our robust free-enterprise system has turned to outsourcing manufacturing overseas, both because the labor is cheaper and also because the US government has strict regulations with lengthy applications and permits that can take years before reaching approval. But I believe this outsourcing of manufacturing to be an American tragedy in the making.

During the pandemic, I was stunned to discover that approximately 90 percent of the medications Americans use, some necessary to sustain life, are imported from foreign countries.[6] When another country controls our vital drugs, we are at their mercy to export them to us. So imagine if we had some conflict with a foreign country from whom we import medical supplies—would Americans be able to get their medications? I would gladly pay a little more to have them made in the US.

The pandemic recently exposed this issue, with face masks and PPE equipment being shipped from overseas. This outsourcing puts

---

6 Andrew Heritage, "Skyrocketing Pharmaceutical Imports to the U.S. Endanger National Security," Coalition for a Prosperous America, January 9, 2023, https://prosperousamerica.org/skyrocketing-pharmaceutical-imports-to-the-u-s-endanger-national-security/.

America in a very dangerous dependent relationship, and so we must incentivize our companies to return to the US. If we want to retain our leadership status in the world, we need to bring American companies back to American soil. But in order to do so, we must first revitalize our approach to career and technical education.

CHAPTER TWO

Improving Education and Training Systems in the US

Educating Counselors, Educators, Parents, and Students on CTE Options—Removing the Stigmas

The American K–12 students are made up of a diverse group of young people. Their interests vary, with emphasis on the arts, science, information technology, business, skilled trades, mathematics, technology, and more. It is the college-prep model that has driven our K–12 educational delivery for years, and the disregarding of CTE illuminates a lack of recognition for the diversity of our student population. Many misconceptions about pursuing CTE exist, and there continues to be an attitude that the only reason a student goes into CTE is because he or she has poor grades, behavioral problems, or attendance issues while attending a traditional school.

But choosing to attend a CTE school does not signal an academic achievement gap. Rather, students traditionally attend trade schools because the programs offered better align with their interests. CTE offers manual, mechanical, academic, and technical challenges. Few colleges offer programs in these areas, even though trade skills are in high demand. For a person seeking to master a technical skill, a four-year university education can be a waste of time.

In an article in *The Atlantic*, Meg St-Esprit discusses these CTE stigmas at length: "College doesn't make sense is the message that many trade schools and apprenticeship programs are using to entice new students. What especially does not make sense, they claim, is the amount of debt many young Americans take on to chase those coveted bachelor's degrees." She goes on to explain that, as of 2020, Americans totaled $1.5 trillion in student debt. She also emphasizes how master's and doctorate degrees typically contribute to even more student loans, but that one's earning potential following this additional education doesn't always return the financial investment. Shockingly, she notes that only two-thirds of degree earners feel their debt was worth it.[7]

The US economy is experiencing a historic shortage of skilled trade people. With skilled trade jobs in high demand, completing technical training is a highly practical and often lucrative option. According to the National Society of High School Scholars, "It is no surprise that the highest-paying trades are in the fields of infrastructure and construction, advanced mechanics, and engineering. Trades in these industries pay at least $50k annually, with demand increasing as few high school students enter trade programs. The eight skilled trades pay the most out of trade school or community college." They go on to say that construction management jobs have a median salary of $98,890 per year, while boilermakers can average up to $84,000. Electricians, who usually spend about two years in trade school, can earn a starting salary of $61,000.[8]

Since the early years of the 21st century, the federal government has recognized the skilled-labor shortage and implemented programs under Presidents Bush, Obama, Trump, and Biden to help mitigate this crisis. CTE offers a pathway for high-skill, high-wage, and high-demand jobs to its students. Career Clusters officially include: Science, Technology, Engineering and Mathematics,

---

7   Meg St-Esprit, "The Stigma of Choosing Trade School Over College," *The Atlantic,* March 6, 2019, https://www.theatlantic.com/education/archive/2019/03/choosing-trade-school-over-college/584275/.

8   Barbara Henry, "Highest Paying Trades," NSHSS, April 29, 2024, https://www.nshss.org/resources/blog/blog-posts/highest-paying-trades/.

Law, Public Safety and Security, Agriculture, Food and Natural Resources, Human Services, Transportation, Distribution and Logistics, Finance, Architecture and Construction, Education and Training, Arts, AV Technology and Communications, Health Sciences, Government and Public Administration, Manufacturing, Business Management and Administration, Marketing Sales and Service, Information Technology, Hospitality and Tourism. The educational players include high schools, community and technical colleges, career centers, four-year universities, and businesses. The career clusters feature high school and postsecondary-enabling career pathways to degrees and certifications. Technical training is integrated with academics in a rigorous and relevant curriculum. Many states are now working on rebranding CTE as an affordable pathway to a well-paying career.[9]

In my experience with rebranding CTE, I was rather amused when one of my colleagues stated that her son wanted to go into the residential-construction CTE program, and his high school counselor told him that he was "too smart" to become "just a builder." He was a high academic achiever and wanted to follow in his grandparents' footsteps to own and manage a construction business. The counselor was unaware that the young man's mother was a CTE instructor. After some angst over him possibly throwing away college scholarships, the counselor finally supported the student's decision to go into the building trades. He went on to be a highly successful residential-building contractor and has continued in this career for twenty-five years. This advice was also given to numerous students that I had instructed at the CTE center. In another incident at a city school, I had an outstanding student in my residential-construction program. He was the valedictorian of his high school class. He shared with me that the counselors and other educators had tried to

---

9   Catrin Wigfall, "State Initiatives Work to Eliminate Lingering Stigma of 'Vocational' Education," American Experiment, March 22, 2018, https://www.americanexperiment.org/state-initiatives-work-to-eliminate-lingering-stigma-of-vocational-education/.

persuade him not to attend the CTE classes and remain on a college-bound track. He was extremely intelligent, and they felt he should go on to college and not waste his intelligence. He is now a highly successful builder in Michigan.

For years, many of us heard from guidance counselors that our students should be on college-bound paths, and that success in life was completing a college education. At a young age, I became a carpenter and cabinetmaker as I trained in my father's business. I then went on to complete my undergraduate work with a BS in industrial education and received my master's degree in career technical education & administration. I have been asked which educational experience I value the most, and the truth is that I value both my career training and postsecondary experiences equally at the highest level of achievement and satisfaction. When I build a beautiful set of cabinets, I can stand back and admire my accomplishment. When I teach a student how to lay out and build a set of stairs for a home and they succeed, I get another great feeling of success in seeing the growth of the student and what it will mean for their future success. For me, success comes from the journey of life, in what makes you feel pride and achievement, no matter which career path you pick.

A young man or woman desiring to go into a residential or commercial-building career has many advantages by attending a two-year residential-construction class in high school, as well as the option of changing his or her mind and attending college instead after high school graduation. For the students who stay in this career technical track, they will receive hands-on experience in building all facets of a home, safety training, employability-skills training, and the like. As these students prepare for high school graduation, they will be immediately employable and receive placement assistance from a placement coordinator and their instructor at the CTE school. Another option for them is to work in the trade (and earn money) as an apprentice and receive a two-year degree at a community college in related training as a carpenter. They would complete basic college coursework, and their employer will often pay for their tuition or a portion of it. Many community colleges are now offering this education free of charge. The student who chooses the career technical track in high school, attends a two-year apprenticeship-studies program in college, and receives on-the-job training will have earned a living, become fully trained, and gained experience in the trade. This makes him or her fully capable of proficiency in their field, becoming a construction manager or construction business owner. Students who complete an apprenticeship, according to the US Department of Labor, will make on average over $300,000 more in their lifetime than those who do not.[10]

Throughout the evolution of education in the US, educators began to recognize that not all students learn in the same manner and some aren't geared for a four-year college track. As a result, more opportunities began to open for students in the 1970s. In Michigan, several secondary technical schools were built to deliver career technical training for high school students, and it was working quite well through the 1990s. Often these high school students would continue their related training at a community college. Unfortunately, the focus on pushing all students to a four-year degree became more intense, and, with many of these facilities failing to attract students for various reasons, the institutions were not producing the needed number of human resources.

Hiring the Best Management, Educators, and Support Staff in Career Technical Education

Because I have been involved in CTE for over forty years, I've gained some insight into this challenging world. Many changes have occurred in CTE, especially over the last twenty-five years in

---

10   "Did You Know?" Homepage, Apprenticeship.gov, effective May 2025, https://www.apprenticeship.gov/.

the requirements for hiring vocational administrators and teachers. The charter and bylaws concerning vocational-career education by the State of Michigan originally suggested that an administrator or director in a career technical facility should be vocationally certified and have taught for three years in a vocational program. There were many reasons for this requirement and the most important one is that by having vocational experience, one could understand what it takes to teach and train young people in a technical field. This practice faded when the state decided that anyone with a degree in educational administration could be hired to operate or manage a CTE center. But CTE schools are vastly different from academic institutions in their structure. Numerous CTE centers in Michigan have hired academic-style administrators to lead the development and management of these facilities. In some cases, the administrators can be trained to do an acceptable job, which usually depends on the support they receive and what career technical knowledge they may have. But unfortunately, some of these administrators are not in touch with the training or what is needed to direct a CTE facility. As a result, unnecessary closure of certain CTE programs is occurring, and unnecessary programs are being installed.

In addition, underqualified technical staff that have not achieved expertise in their field are being hired. For example, it is very difficult to find a fully qualified expert in construction technology with many years of experience and training that also has a four-year teaching degree. Someone at the level of this expertise would be making a six-figure-plus income and have little incentive to take a lower-paying job in education. Because it's difficult to find fully qualified technical educators, there is real concern surrounding the safety of training students. Many programs use extremely dangerous equipment, and hiring a teacher who has not had the proper experience and safety training can put the instructor and students at risk. Unfortunately, some CTE administrators have countered this issue by scaling back hands-on training in order to reduce their own liability. But programs with reduced hands-on training cannot properly prepare students for expertise in their chosen career.

The current educational establishment requires that, to become a vocational educator, a person should have a four-year teaching degree and have either worked in a technical occupation for over four years, or have two thousand hours of recent training and experience in that technical field. However, for many fields, two thousand hours is not enough to fully master the knowledge and expertise in the skill. For years, highly skilled career technical instructors were recruited from industry, received annual authorization to teach, and were encouraged to go back to college and become recognized as a certified educator.[11]

Eventually, this became a requirement at the CTE center where I was employed in the 1980s. For many of the technical educators, this was a hard pill to swallow. While most instructors did follow through with a college teaching certification, we lost a number of outstanding educators as well. The educators that remained went on to college and finished a four-year teaching degree, many going even further and completing a master's degree. Continued teacher-education classes are required to maintain teacher certification. Many instructors in technical trades have at least four years of college education plus time in the field working on their skills. Some universities were producing technically trained staff for several years in the 1980s and '90s, but many have cut back on these programs. Now, it is even harder to recruit someone from the industry to teach, obtain a four-year teaching degree, and have him or her agree to a possible pay cut. Because of these requirements, it has become difficult to find well-rounded and fully competent technical educators.

What would make the most practical sense is to continue having "Annual Career Authorization" and work with community colleges or

---

11   "Annual Career Authorization," Michigan Department of Education, effective May 2025, https://www.michigan.gov/mde/services/ed-serv/ed-cert/permits-placement/annual-career-authorization.

four-year colleges to offer a shortened version of teacher-certification classes. The tuition should be free of charge for those working under annual authorization and the curriculum should offer courses in teaching strategies, safety, developing lesson plans, classroom management, and formulating student assessments. Recent work experience continues to be an important ticket toward certification, and many colleges offer credits for work experience. The Michigan Department of Education has clarified the guidelines of "recent and relevant" work experience directly related to the CTE area. [12]

While I was working on and developing the work-based learning program, some of my colleagues were working on a career-development component. It was this component that got me excited as well, because I knew that if we were going to fine-tune our apprenticeship program, we needed to educate students much earlier in their K–12 schooling. In other words, we needed to implement a comprehensive career component that started from kindergarten and ran through grade ten. This component would have a series of required markers, such as academic assessments and career-exploration opportunities, for students to achieve to prepare themselves for the world of work. This is what education and training are supposed to do! After education and training, we should all theoretically be able to get a job and contribute to society through work.

The Impact of Family Support and Early Education on Our System

Humans are constantly learning about their environment from birth, and many studies have shown that the human mind has the greatest capacity to learn when we're born. Since the malleability of our brains is at the highest when young and slowly begins to drop as we grow and mature, it stands to reason that we need to begin the educational process as early as we can with our early learners.

---

12   Michigan Department of Education, "Annual Career Authorization."

Over the years I have been involved in many aspects of education, and I was deeply touched by my involvement with our local chamber years ago. I sat on the Grand Rapids Chamber of Commerce committee for about three years as an educator and got involved with the literacy program. I had the opportunity to work with many of our districts in the Kent County area to pull data and talk with hundreds of parents and educators on this subject. I even had the opportunity to evaluate many of the local programs. In looking at our local schools and their programs, I compared districts that were having the most success. I wanted to know why they were so successful and why their students did well consistently. After much research and discussion, it became obvious. The students in these districts had parents, grandparents, and mentors that were engaged in their education. There were strong family values at home. Some may conclude that these students came from affluent parents who had a higher income or status. For a very small percentage of kids this may be true, but, for the most part, the reason that these children had success was because they had a caring and supportive family that was engaged with their children daily.

During my last few years as an educator, I had the opportunity to work with the inner-city schools where many students were not from affluent families. Here, it became even more evident to me that the success of the student was directly correlated to the amount of stability, interaction, and concern he or she received at home.

One of the first things young people learn is how to talk and read. When children begin on their educational path, it is quite different for each of them. Studies and personal experiences have shown that children who are read to at an early age and taught to read early on are much more successful and achieve higher levels than students who are not read to. I experienced this with my youngest daughter. At the time she was born, I was researching this information. I focused on reading with her every night before bedtime. By the time she was four years old, she had an excellent grasp of language and began reading herself.

She went on to complete college and achieved at the higher end of the educational scale. I had read to all my children, but for this child, it was a concentrated effort on my part.

The best way to improve our educational system is to start with the families of young preschool children. Currently, the cost to send four-year-olds to pre-K classes is approximately $2,000 at most public schools. Pre-K education is vital, and so we should be investing as much money as possible in the early years of *all* our children's education. It shouldn't just be available to those who can afford it. This will help balance the playing field for all children, not just for children who have parents better off financially. After all, once a child starts out on the wrong foot, it is very hard to help them catch up and compete with students who received early education. By providing all kids with an equal start, we will save our society billions of dollars in cost for special programs that remediate students year after year. Implementing free preschool would correct a big part of the educational delivery system.

One of the latest educational trends is about charter schools, private schools, and schools of choice. The reason students may be more successful in the above-mentioned institutions is not because of socioeconomic reasons or the fact that one school spends more money per student. Rather, it's family involvement with the child that makes the difference. Our traditional public schools would flourish if all students had support from family at home, people personally invested in their student's education. The other disturbing point I would like to make about schools of choice is the fact that it is causing segregation in our schools. All the charter or schools of choice are filled with mostly white students, and most of the minority students are being left behind in a struggling public school. Part of this issue is transportation. Let's say, in a schools-of-choice scenario, that all parents in a certain area are allotted the same amount of money for their children. But if some parents don't have a way to transport their child to the other district, then only the students with transportation options will be able to attend anyway. This needs to change.

For a successful education system, the US needs to infuse more money into strengthening families and in the early development stages of our children. Along with some of the early changes with preschool, we need to make sure each school in the K–12 system has implemented a full career-development process that engages students in exploring all facets of our business and industry workforce.

MISCONCEPTIONS IN EDUCATIONAL ATTAINMENT AND WAGES

Our educational system is controlled and influenced by higher education. This is not done directly, but by setting high standards that students be accepted into and attend postsecondary institutions. This part of the K–12 academic track has been flourishing for decades, but a much better job needs to be done directing students into their prospective career paths. This can be accomplished by exposing our youth to diverse careers at a much younger age and helping them interact with many of the career-assessment tools that exist today.

Training and educating our school counselors is still a big issue. In Kent County, we started this process of collaborating with counselors over thirty years ago, but once we stopped, the system seemed to flex back to its original posture. Many counselors are back to recommending the four-year college track as the most successful, even though our data speaks differently. Higher education is partly to blame, as these institutions promote literature showing the earning differences between those with a college degree and those with only a high school diploma. They are correct in stating that degree earners make more, because students who are trained and educated after high school do earn more money; however, students who go on to a community college and complete related training for the apprenticeship certificate often make very nice incomes, per data collected by the US Department of Labor. I have combined data from the National Center for Education Statistics and the US Department of Labor to show an actual comparison for the entire educational system, as seen in the chart on page 24 . According to this broader scope of data, the average salary for an apprentice is outperforming many of the four-year degree programs and some of the master's degree programs.[13] This data doesn't align with the typical postsecondary message, especially when higher education receives billions of dollars from our federal government each year.

Many students who complete their college coursework for their apprenticeship certificate may not have enough credits for an associate's degree. Some do take the remaining classes, but not all do. So, many of these students are in the comparison. Higher education is discriminating against this group of people. The coordinators that were hired by the ISD in Michigan during this period spent a good share of time informing the local counselors of some of the other options for students to be successful, especially in the technical fields. It is true that many of the professional jobs that require four, five, or even up to eight years of education pay well, but as you can see, many of the apprenticeship students are making a much higher salary than the four-year-degreed students.[14]

---

13   "Annual Earnings by Educational Attainment," Condition of Education, National Center for Education Statistics, last updated May 2024, https://nces.ed.gov/programs/coe/indicator/cba.

14   National Center for Education Statistics, "Annual Earnings by Educational Attainment."

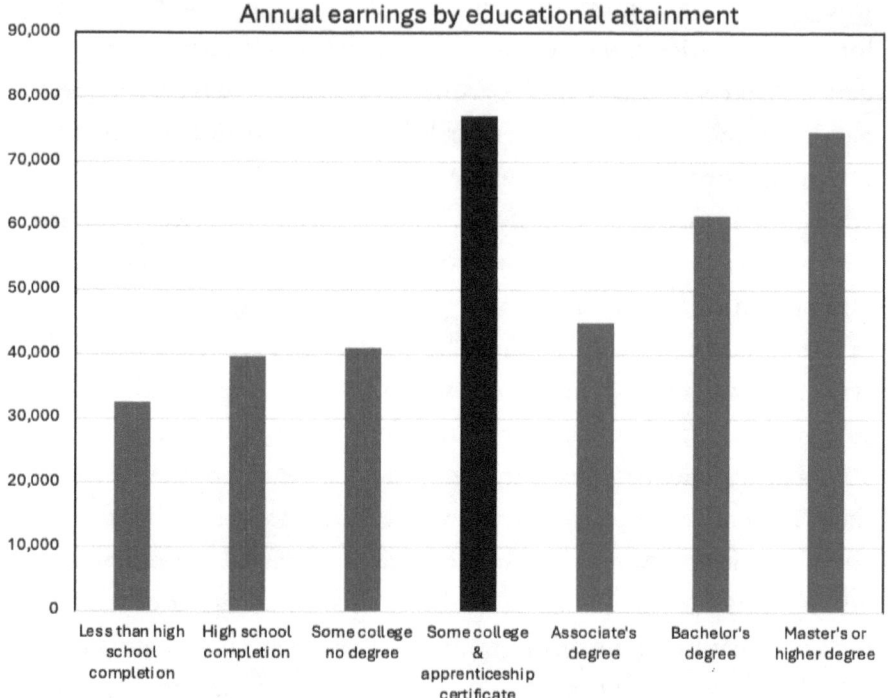

The above graph is a blend of information that was disclosed by the National Center of Education and Statistics[15] and the US Department of Labor.[16]

Note: Data is based on sample surveys of the noninstitutionalized population, which excludes persons living in institutions (e.g., prison or nursing facilities) and military barracks. Full-time, year-round workers are those who worked thirty-five hours per week for fifty or more weeks per year.[17]

---

15 "Postsecondary Institution Revenues," Condition of Education, National Center for Education Statistics, last updated August 2023, https://nces.ed.gov/programs/coe/indicator/cud.
16 Apprenticeship.gov, "Did You Know?"
17 "Current Population Survey: 2022 Annual Social and Economic (ASEC) Supplement," United States Census Bureau, effective May 2025, https://www2.census.gov/programs-surveys/cps/techdocs/cpsmar22.pdf.

From the gathered data I was able to deduce that American apprenticeship personnel have an average salary of $77,000 per year at the end of their training. In addition, employment retention is 93 percent nationwide, and apprentice graduates earn more over their lifetime compared to their non-apprentice peers.[18] This information is significant and noteworthy, considering the status of our educational system, and it's exactly why we need to retool our American educational plan.

Another misconception commonly perpetuated in our society is that success only comes with a four-year college education. But not all students are four-year-college bound, and many people do not realize what it takes to go through and complete an apprenticeship program. The related training courses attached to the apprenticeship programs are highly technical and take an elevated level of academic achievement to succeed. Every apprenticeship program that I've worked with had postsecondary education attached to it. In fact, all apprenticeship programs have 576 hours minimum of postsecondary training or education as part of the program, besides field or applied training. Many of the more advanced technical trades are now a part of five- or six-year programs. We need to teach students that they cannot get by with only a high school diploma—if college isn't right for them, they will need some form of vocational training alongside postsecondary education to be successful in the middle class and above.

This, then, is why we need to develop a technical track for students alongside our current academic track, and this process needs to start much earlier than it does currently. Those high school juniors fortunate enough to get into a technical program at a CTE center are blessed. They can connect with an employer and a job, then complete their education or technical training at one of their community colleges.

It is the employer who currently bears most of the support for this system, and changes are needed to help our employers and workforce compete in this global economy. It must become a national effort

---

18 Apprenticeship.gov, "Did You Know?"

to provide financial support for apprenticeship programs, because business and industry cannot continue paying for most of this system and expect to be competitive in the global market. Today, students should be allowed to develop career technical skills and knowledge while in high school. That's why many CTE centers were built in Michigan, to help in the education and training for those who either did not want to go on to college or could not afford it. These CTE centers shorten students' time spent preparing for their careers and provide employers with a prepared technical workforce much earlier in the process.

CHAPTER THREE

Is the Educational Environment Open or Closed?

The present K–12 American educational structure has developed a solid system. However, because of the current pace of life, including the many complexities of work, family, and governmental controls, the system has been slowly changing. Our schools in the past were an open and inclusive environment, but as time has passed and the size of schools has increased, so has the complexity of the operation of these schools.

Along with teaching for many years, I also sat on one of the local school boards for five years. This has helped me to understand a bit more about the operation of the school's environment. It was not until I worked out of the career technical center and spent some time on the school board that I realized schools prefer to work from within, and they're not that interested in getting input from the outside. As a result, I would say many of these institutions are "closed," rarely allowing for external input to assist in the growth of the system. Don't get me wrong here—there are many partnerships I have noted around the country where parents and businesses are engaged, but they are rare. Company employees may assist as tutors and interact with the students, but there is rarely an employer that is welcomed to help a math teacher deliver math in a skill-related and more understandable way. Not much of this type of input is occurring. I have been involved in vocational programs in Wyoming, Michigan, and across the country that had employer advisory committees. I have participated in many of these committees over the years and have witnessed directly how often the input simply becomes a "rubber stamp" on administrative agendas.

For example, in the 1990s, I was on a special team that was put together by our director of CTE. Our mission at that time was the implementation of the Applied-Technology Curriculum Model. This team of educators researched, assembled, and wrote a document that was designed to assist the many local districts with core academics, educational-development plans, and technology education, and it had a work-based learning component as part of the delivery system. Our job was to convince the local districts that by implementing these programs, students would be better prepared for the 21st century job and career market. My job as part of the team was to develop the work-based learning component, which included career visits and apprenticeships with employers, job shadowing, mentorships, internships, and co-ops. During partnership development, I connected with several very influential CEOs in our community. I will not name them, but several of these companies are known nationally, and their CEOs believed that helping to implement these programs in the local districts would not only help career technical students, but that it would be great for all students in the county.

I discovered from personal experience that our educational system had become a closed environment, and the local CTE administrators felt like they would lose control over their career-educational systems if they allowed the input of these influential CEOs. We have seen this same closed approach with school boards across the country when parents are blocked from giving input. This may not be true of all learning institutions across the country, but the general trend toward this closed mindset is alarming.

As a teacher, life is very fast-paced, and for many educators, each day brings numerous decisions that have to be dealt with and executed throughout the day. Because of this, many teachers do not get involved with everyday educational politics or administrative issues such as truancy policy. As a result, it is hard to understand the larger impact that forces from the outside community have on the day-to-day school environment. In the late 1980s, I ran for the school board in the district that I was living in. After moving back to Michigan from Wyoming, I noted that in Wyoming we had a 20:1 student-to-teacher ratio, carpeted schools, swimming pools, and plenty of computers per student. I was shocked that my own children were coming into a district in Michigan that had a 30:1 student-to-teacher ratio, few computers per student, old desks, old schools, and old floors. I felt like I needed to engage with my district to see if something could be done to upgrade students' education. This was my first reality check, confirming that it's just not that easy to change an educational system.

At that time, in my current job, I had been put on a team that was trying to change some of the old paradigms in education and introduce new approaches and curriculum regionally to assist teachers in making a larger impact on students. As we found with our team, it would not be an easy task to change a system that had been in place for years. However, we did learn that by using current existing research, compiling our own research, and taking one step at a time, it was possible to slowly change the system and have a dramatic impact on overall education quality. After a couple of years, our team felt that we were making a difference in the local districts; however, for some of us on the team, change wasn't coming fast enough.

Many of us on the team were looking for new ways to expand our message. For me, a lot of my work was within the business community, and I would be running into new business owners daily. One very significant person that I became acquainted with was a man named Ron. He was a company owner who had a degree in systems theory and was a pastor of a local church. Ron was involved with several highly influential local CEOs in Grand Rapids, Kent County, and the surrounding areas. Ron had listened to my brief presentation regarding all the programs and activities that we were involved in, and he was excited about the student opportunities. Curious to see more, he sat in on the apprenticeship committee that I had put together to assist us in moving young people into local apprenticeship programs with employers. I asked Ron to speak at one of our training workshops, and he talked about systems theory and how it was related to our work as an educational institution. It was received very well by our business partners and educators alike.

After a few days had passed, Ron called and said he had a proposal for me regarding help for the Applied-Technology team. He said he could help spread our message much faster, and I was thrilled at this news. We met, and Ron proposed his idea: He had recruited approximately ten of the top CEOs in the local area for what he called a "blue-ribbon commission." The commission would make presentations to the local educators sharing their support for our efforts and explaining what their apprenticeships would offer. I was giddy with excitement! I had spent around three years pounding the streets trying to convince key players that our mission was great for students and businesses alike, and Ron's offer seemed like the answer to all of our prayers at once.

I told Ron that I had to clear it with our CTE director, but I told him that I thought it would be well received since we had been directed to convince educators and businesses of our educational agenda. I called our director, asked to meet with him, and relayed that I had great news regarding the business community's projected involvement with our educational objectives. Our director was a brilliant man with great creativity and vision for CTE. The Applied-Technology Model was his brainchild, and I had and still have the utmost respect for him. I went in and sat down with the director and told him about Ron's proposal. As I did, he must have noticed my excitement. After explaining and telling him about the proposal, I saw a blank look come over his face, and then there was a long pause. He looked at me and said, "No"—we could not let them put a blue-ribbon commission together.

I was stunned. When I asked why not, he said that we would not be able to control them and their involvement in our educational system. I was shocked, stunned, and disappointed. I felt like all our hard work was for nothing. It was with great regret that I had to inform these amazing partners that we could not take them up on their most gracious offer.

During the next fifteen years, I came to the simple conclusion that while the educational system wants to make it *look* like they're open to partnership and input, they actually intend on controlling every aspect internally. I saw this theme in our advisory committees as well, where the business community was trumped by many of the educators who sat on these committees with them. Whether this position comes from teacher unions or educational administrators, it destroys the integrity of our promise to provide excellence and opportunities for our youth.

I've come full circle with the realization that the education system talks a good game, but often fails to deliver when it comes to full disclosure, transparency, and cooperation. Therefore, I argue that education is a closed environment, and this is something that must change. We need transparency and cooperation with business, parents, and community for the benefit of our students.

As a lifelong educator, I have witnessed firsthand that the differences between public, private, and charter schools don't come down to money. Students in all three environments see success. Instead, it's their family that often makes the difference. I have worked in each one of these systems, and when parents are engaged in their child's education, that child's success is almost guaranteed.

The concept that simply throwing more taxpayer money at a problem will solve things is aggravating to me. We can increase the overall government investment per student, but if the family support system is not engaged with their child and their learning, we can continue to expect lower student scores for that child. Throwing taxpayer money at educational problems cannot produce better outcomes unless true change is implemented. When parents promote schools of choice or charter schools, they do not truly understand why private or charter schools might be testing higher than public schools. It's not because these schools have better teachers or more spending per pupil—it's the attention, involvement, and concern of family members and mentors.

One of my last teaching assignments as an educator was to work with troubled youth at an inner-city school in Grand Rapids, Michigan. It was an "alternative ed" program for students that had been suspended from regular high school. I had a diverse group of students from varied races and ethnicities. At parent-teacher conferences, I noted that rarely did two parents and often not even one parent or grandparent attend. The students who *did* have a parent or two show up tended to be the ones who excelled in their academics and extracurriculars. Many of these students with family involvement have gone on to engage in life with great success.

So, for me, to hear and see people pushing to destroy public education because of overall testing scores is devastating. Instead, we need to put our efforts into strengthening the families and support systems of our youth, and we can't keep closing off our educational system from family involvement. How can we expect families to support their children if their input isn't valued in the educational setting?

Whether isolated from the family or local businesses, education's current closed approach is hurting our students in the long run.

CHAPTER FOUR

Developing Partnerships Between Business, Industry, and Education

Partnerships play an enormous role in the development of our educational system. Business and industry are at the final step of a supply-and-demand, customer-based educational system. When I was part of the Applied-Technology team, one of the goals was to ensure team members were trained in systems theory. Probably the one thing that stuck out the most for me was the importance of the customer. A major stumbling block when it comes to servicing customers is understanding who the customers are in the first place. You need to understand who they are before you can even think about fulfilling their needs.

We, in education, are producing or supplying a "product" called the student. And, if our product—the student—finishes as a highly prepared individual, then our customer—the employer—prospers. We then would have completed our purpose as an educational institution in delivering a positive outcome, and the cycle continues.

This is why our educational system is currently failing for half of our population. We have pushed for students to pursue higher education so much that we have ignored a large percentage of the student population for whom this isn't viable. Many employers in the technical areas are always looking for good talent to fulfill their many diverse jobs. This problem exists because we have gotten off course with producing a product that our customer wants. Schools are pushing a one-track system, one that neglects potential technical-track students, and this needs to stop. This is why we need to develop a technical track at the high school level. Fewer of our students are prepared to work in career technical areas because our school system is not focused on this area. Many students have been steered away from CTE classes and then flounder after graduating or dropping out of college. Some eventually go into a career technical area but have wasted money and a few good years of the most productive parts of their lives. Plus, companies in the last two decades have moved manufacturing to foreign countries to lower their labor costs. Many of our technically trained people are retiring, and there are not enough trained younger people to fill this void. It is for this reason that the system must be altered to better prepare our pool of human resources. Do I sound like a broken record? I hope so, because we *need* to improve our current educational system if we want to meet the demands of our society and our country today.

A combined effort must emerge to develop an equal degree of funding for CTE and academic universities. We will need a small amount of restructuring for the educational side, along with the government's input from the Bureau of Apprenticeship and Training (BAT) as well as the management side of industry for the apprenticeship system. Many partnerships will have to be solidified to make this a successful collaboration. This is the key for developing an equally recognized Y-track system that is balanced for the supply-and-demand nature of the job market. By achieving this Y-track, we will effectively utilize our human resources in the US and help our innovative employers become more competitive in the global market.

Each educational facility will need a coordinator to support the partnerships needed in this ideal system. Most apprenticeships are held within the employer's place of business, and so it will take a combined effort on the part of the educators and employers to provide a bridge so that information can flow back and forth. I did this type of coordination for fifteen years, and we were very close to establishing the perfect system. With a balanced flow of money from the local, state, and federal government, we can finalize a system that flourishes. But it will take a concerted effort on behalf of the employer, the K–12 educational system, and the US Department of Labor as well as the Bureau of Apprenticeship and Training.

The four people that are key to this system are 1) a BAT representative, 2) a K–12 school-to-apprenticeship coordinator, 3) a community college apprenticeship coordinator, and 4) the apprenticeship company's HR person. Time and effort must be allotted to establish both the human and financial resources needed to support this type of system. This system is nearly complete today. However, we need to recognize the CTE track that would operate alongside the higher-ed track. Today, the funding is not equally distributed, and I am sure that the higher-education forces will resist splitting the funding they receive.

There are several ways that partnerships can be developed. Early on, I started with cold-calling employers and asking them about their employment needs. I also developed flyers that we could send to employers asking them if they had any certified training programs that they hosted or supported. In addition, we sponsored an industry expo each year. We would invite approximately sixty to seventy employers and have display tables set up for them. The students would roam around in the expo and talk to potential employers about what they had to offer and what they expected from the employee. This was done in the early spring as many of our students were getting to the end of their technical training and were approaching job interviews. Students who presented themselves well received an early interview, especially if the employer was looking for a new hire. We also had students whose employer co-op programs were coming to an end and were hoping to turn their positions into full-time apprenticeships. Several companies preferred to start with co-ops because they felt less obligated to commit and weren't locked into apprenticeship agreements with students right away. However, many of the companies soon began to realize the quality of talent we were producing and later accepted more students into apprenticeship agreements.

Some companies did the full gamut by running a sort of linear Apprenticeship-Development Program, allowing our younger students to start out with job shadowing. Then as those students got older, they would be offered internship opportunities, which later turned into co-ops or even full-fledged apprenticeships. At the end of our program, we had most of these students that participated in the interaction between businesses come out of the Apprenticeship-Development Program. However, we did have some students that failed to sign up in the fall and later changed their minds about their future direction. In this case, we would make several attempts to assess them and connect them with an employer for an apprenticeship related to their program of training.

People have a wide variety of views on what a partnership with business and industry is and how it should look. For me, I tried to look at it from the perspective that any interaction between our local industry and education, big or small, was significant. Whether we had a full-scale apprenticeship going with the employer, mock interviews, or just a small job-shadowing program, it all mattered. Something as small as businesses talking to students about their industry made a big difference.

Referring to the career brochure that we had developed for K–12 education explains it all. Students and business/industry must interact continuously to have a healthy partnership that will allow the system to grow and prosper. As a placement coordinator for fifteen years, I can tell you from pounding the streets that there should be two or three career or placement coordinators per school to handle the work that will need to be done to support a dual Y-track system. Because we are housed in a regional tech center, we can handle approximately 50–150 students in the manufacturing and technical areas per year. This sounds like a low number, but each student requires thorough time and attention, including reviewing all the paperwork for state-approved work permits and training agreements, performing site visits to the employers, and communicating between the instructors and employer staff.

Just think about this type of system and what can be accomplished. Students can move from high school to a full-time job as an apprentice, which often leads to a lifelong career. The system will take them to the community college to further their academic education as part of their related training for their apprenticeship. They will start out at approximately 50 percent of what a journeyman makes. In most cases, their starting wages are at or above seventeen to twenty-two dollars per hour and are progressive depending on the number of hours and completed classes. When we operated our program, students who were enrolled in the school-to apprenticeship path would receive academic credit for one thousand hours of work time. This also helped them achieve a higher pay wage by the time they graduated, and allowed them to graduate from the apprenticeship training earlier than normal with full journeyman status.

CHAPTER FIVE

Union vs. Nonunion Workforces and the Impact of Right-to-Work Legislation on the Current Apprenticeship System

There has been controversial debate regarding the "right-to-work" legislation as it relates to our workforce and training systems. This legislation was designed to keep employees from being forced to join a union, and I believe that this is fundamentally good. However, there are consequences regarding policies like this, and there are different views on the topic from both legislators and the public.

As previously stated, I was first employed as a carpenter in a nonunion business. Although it was a family-operated business, I had no recourse if I did not like the working conditions. I learned quickly that, in this system, I received better working conditions as I went up the ladder. After returning to college and acquiring a degree, I began teaching in a residential-construction program in a public school. This organization had a union, so I got my first introduction to unionized work. The first thing I disliked about the union was the fact that I had to join—there was no choice in the matter. And, of course, being part of a union requires payment of dues. I later worked for two other organizations that were also unionized. These various experiences gave me a taste of both worlds.

Currently, numerous states are passing laws to allow right-to-work legislation, and people need to understand how this will impact themselves and their workplace. But first we need to understand why unions exist at all. In the eighteenth century, many areas around the country started to become increasingly industrialized. In these industrial settings, young workers were taken advantage of by long hours, low wages, and poor working conditions. Over the years, more and more companies have become unionized to compromise with better wages and conditions. Conditions slowly improved for workers over time, and along with better wages and safety practices, management wanted to help improve training. In conjunction with the unions, businesses started providing much of employee training, elevating themselves through a well-organized and well-educated workforce.

In 1937 the Davis–Bacon Act helped with the early beginnings of the American apprenticeship system. Over time, with the help of our local community colleges and the Bureau of Apprenticeship and Training, a documented system began to emerge. Through this system the American middle class was born, and it flourished. In the 1980s our country slowly began to change. From a national outcry regarding "overpopulation," people were encouraged to have smaller families and fewer children. In earlier years, young people got into apprenticeships by knowing a relative or family friend that could train them. Often, apprenticeship jobs were handed down from father to son, and as there were fewer sons available, a shortage began to emerge in many of the apprenticeship programs. There was a push to recruit more people, including minorities and nontraditional workers, to fill the growing gaps.

Along with this came the information age, and increased technology began to change the job landscape. Because of the advent of robotics, for example, many people felt that workers in the welding field would soon be replaced by robots. Robotics did work for some of the automotive assembly lines and small, repetitive jobs, but for other jobs around the country, such as the construction of steel high-rise buildings, trailer manufacturing, and small craft-type jobs, it soon became apparent that only humans could perform such intricate work. With humans continuing their critical work in these trades, unions are still highly relevant today.

When we vote for a right-to-work state, just what are we getting? If the vote is adopted, one may have a job, but it will be a job that is smaller in scope, has very little technical skill required, and very little training associated. What does that mean? Under a union plan, one is trained over a four-year period, and at the end of their training they have a transferable skill that they can take to any state with a formal apprenticeship program and receive similar wages. In a right-to-work state, one may be paid less. And with minimal skill, they would be easily replaceable. Though they'd be working, their ability to support a family would be questionable.

Let me give you another example of the union versus nonunion formats. I taught at a community college for a period of nine years. My students were enrolled in a carpentry apprenticeship program, and I had students from two organizations, Associated Builders and Contractors (ABC) and Associated General Contractors (AGC). Instead of union dues, the ABC organization has membership fees. They support the right-to-work legislation, which allows their members not to join if they so choose. However, if you're not paying the membership fees, you're more likely to be passed over regarding internal training within the apprenticeship system. Once a member of ABC, if you paid your membership fees, you would receive apprenticeship training and a series of discounts set up for members throughout their tenure with the company and with ABC. With the merit-shop climate, employers can be more competitive in their contract bidding. This allows the contractors to stay busier year-round. One advantage of the merit-shop system is that small groups can work with management to resolve issues internally without the threat of a strike or shutdown. Because of the structure of the merit-base system, they can provide training at a cheaper cost, which allows them to be more competitive in the open-bidding market.

In comparison, the AGC group has a more traditional approach regarding the union sector of our workforce. Many companies affiliated with AGC that have a traditional union tend to have higher wages and higher costs. These accrued costs make it harder for the companies to be competitive in the open market. For this reason, it has been harder for union contractors to keep steady work on a year-round basis.

Many of our unions have become corrupt. They collect large amounts of money and then look for outside areas to use it. Much of it goes to lobbyists, involving unions in the political arena and not helping the people directly. If the membership could come together and manage the unions in a responsible way, their value would be insurmountable. Union bosses and management need to be paid less, and union dues should benefit the working people, not the union management. A possible solution to this problem is restricting the amount of money that can be used for political lobbying. For teacher unions, for example, 80 percent of dues could go toward education and training purposes, such as early-reading programs and career development. Then 10 percent could go toward management, 5 percent toward curriculum improvement, and 5 percent for political purposes. This would help the teachers by putting their union dues directly to work and boosting overall success for students at the beginning of the educational journey. This would also help many of the educational initiatives become more focused on the individual student. The same would be true for the unions associated with the manufacturing sector. By putting 80 percent back into the apprenticeship-training system, 10 percent for safety and working conditions, and 10 percent for management, those paying the dues would benefit from improved training, in turn making the company more competitive and profitable. Many of these costs should be split between the local, state, and federal government, and all academic funding should be split fifty-fifty between higher and technical education. That would be for all the related training provided throughout high school as well as community college.

To sum it all up, the American middle class was developed and molded by the participation of unions and organized labor. The presence of unions is one of the most important factors in creating a middle class of people that are highly trained and skilled, and it sits at the core of our workforce. When the technically trained apprentices thrive, then our middle class thrives, and the four-year-college-degreed class will thrive as well.

Let me give you one simple example. As a tool and die maker begins their apprenticeship, they are paid approximately one-half the typical wages of a full journeyman. If the journeyman's average wage is forty dollars an hour, the apprentice starts out at around twenty dollars an hour. As this young worker becomes more skilled and increases their education, they're paid more. This process continues until they are fully trained. They will not be in debt for their education, rather they will earn a wage and receive their training at the same time. At the end of this apprenticeship-training process, the beginning journeyman would make approximately $77,000 per year, according to national averages,[19] and he or she would be equipped to support a family and live in the middle class.

This in turn supports our entire system, including some government programs through taxes. We cannot have 80 percent of citizens working in the medical profession or 90 percent of our people working in the service sector of our economy and expect the system to flourish. It's all tied together, and for the system to run smoothly and be successful, the middle class must be large and in charge. For this to happen, strong leadership must make a concerted effort to implement the apprenticeship system into the mainstream of our current educational system. This is the challenge of our society for the 21st century. If we maximize the human potential of our country, we will flourish. If we fail, we will flounder and struggle to survive as a country and as leaders in the free world. In putting the Y-track system in place, we can maximize our human resources, make our companies more competitive at home and globally, and assist in

---

19 Apprenticeship.gov, "Did You Know?"

making our higher education more streamlined and more targeted for every individual in America.

The Y-track system can be easily integrated into our educational system. If America truly wants to have a right-to-work state, and wants to eliminate the unions, then our training system will have to be funded by the overall educational system. Business and industry cannot afford to foot the bill for all this training and still be competitive in the global economy.

CHAPTER SIX

Once Upon a Time in Our Educational System — How Close We Were to the Perfect Dual-Track Delivery System

Early in my educational experience I became involved in a compilation of processes and events for a school-improvement directive. This took place in a CTE center in Michigan that served schools in Kent County. It was our mission to address the educational shortcomings that our district's students were facing in the 1990s. We discovered through research that US students were falling behind in all areas of educational achievement in the world standing. It was the goal of our CTE director to assemble a group of knowledgeable people with expertise in areas related to technical and academic education to research and develop strategies to address many of the shortcomings that students were facing.

Before returning to Michigan to be closer to my family and finish my master's degree, I had been employed as a residential-building instructor in the state of Wyoming. I was then hired as a building-trades instructor at a technical center in Grand Rapids, where I worked for two years. Our CTE director was in the process of hiring a team of educators to research current trends and programs and implement an Applied-Technology Curriculum Model for school improvement. I was hired and took on the position of placement coordinator to develop the office of work-based learning at our technical center. I found this position exciting and challenging, and I believed we could make a difference in our educational system.

The Applied-Technology Curriculum Model had several components that addressed some of the weaknesses in education that were found either through national research studies or by local research we had collected. The components of the model when we started were career education, technology education, and work-based learning. Each of the three components were staffed by an educator who had expertise in the specific area. I was personally responsible for work-based learning. The technology-education aspect included a new curriculum that was assembled as a joint venture with the Ohio and Michigan Departments of Education.

Later we added applied academics, including an applied-math series that came from Texas, principles in technology, some of the sciences, as well as problem-solving and critical-thinking skills. The basic concept was to help students make better career decisions, support their career-development activities, improve their academic abilities, and set them up with a comprehensive set of work-based learning tools. My goal was to place students into one of the high-tech jobs within our community that had formalized training and education components, such as an apprenticeship system.

When I began working in this program, all instructors throughout our center were individually responsible to visit twenty employers per year to place their own students. Some programs operated with a worksite permit that allowed students to go on site. When I became the work-based learning coordinator, I dropped the worksite component to add a stronger "co-op" component. My job was to place recommended students from each of the individual programs throughout the center. All student placements went through my office. Later, I added many more career processes, such as mentorships, internships, job shadowing, and finally a strong apprenticeship component. This became one of the strongest work-based learning models in the country for technical centers and connected a great number of young people into the high-tech job market. Even when the economy struggled, we still managed to place young men and women into the job market through the apprenticeship system.

Besides the three of us that were hired for these specific areas, the team included the assistant director and the CTE director. We, as a team, would meet each morning to discuss the direction and purpose of our goals as well as narrow down our focus on many of the activities that we would attack each day and week. It was at this time that the career center adopted the site license for some of the core curriculum that was developed in Texas. Applied math was one of the areas that we targeted to implement into the local districts. A certified math teacher was hired at that time to head up the math component. Another person was hired to help with technology issues and to assist me in supporting the ever-expanding work-based learning program.

As things progressed over time, we worked with different people from the local districts, including teachers, counselors, administrators, and many organizations from the community and state. Many workshops were developed and put on by our staff. We hosted several conferences and brought in multiple national speakers and experts for motivational and educational purposes.

This was a very exciting time to be involved with education. We were on the cutting edge of changing some of the old paradigms about education, and from much of the research that we had collected, we knew that we were on target with these changes. Some of the changes that we spawned in the local districts included a move to block scheduling, more career-development activities (including the first computerized EDP—Educational Development Plan), and the implementation of the applied-math series into the local districts. We proposed changes to the old industrial-technology programs, incorporating more science, math, and critical-thinking skills in order to help students explore many new technologies, including robotics. As students moved through their education programs, they interacted more with local business and industry, exposing them to more career opportunities. This was accomplished by participating in career events such as field trips, industry talks, job-shadowing activities, mentorships, co-ops, and later an employer-driven apprenticeship program.

After a few years, each part of the Applied-Technology Curriculum Model grew larger and larger until we became individual departments or programs. My group moved from the Kent ISD building into the CTE center. Once we moved and began to focus on the specific tasks at hand, we found ourselves growing again. Two more people were added to assist with the delivery of services that we were attempting to provide in the work-based learning department. By having four coordinators in my office, we then could divide the technical center into four sections based on programs. I continued to work with the technical programs with the most apprenticeship activity, mainly because of the work that I had previously performed with the State of Michigan. As our office became more engaged with the instructors and programs, student activity began to soar. Besides general placement activity, each counselor or coordinator took on the responsibility of providing career-assessment exploration as well as setting up job-shadowing and internship activities for students with employers.

It soon became evident to me that some of the students I was referring to employers were having difficulty in securing or maintaining the job once hired. I felt it was necessary to test the students' academics as soon as I began to work with them to find out if, in fact, these students had the ability to succeed in the academic side of their prospective job. For many of these students, a high level of math and reading were required, and some students were failing due to underdeveloped academic abilities or maturity levels.

As I pondered how to resolve the maturity-level issue, I analyzed how young people become more responsible. I thought back on my own experiences as a young boy working for my father's construction business. At job sites, I worked beside men from twenty to sixty years old. After my initial rite of passage with the construction workers, the crews were very helpful with teaching me skills. The experience of working, talking, and learning from the people around me was significant for my maturity and skill development. I concluded that organizing several meaningful events rigid with both timelines and purpose would indeed help these students with proper protocols.

So, I embarked on developing a process called the Apprenticeship-Development Program. Along with the daily routines of the placement activity and the apprenticeship program, the team of seven coordinators held many activities with the local districts, such as workshops and conferences related to the Applied-Technology Curriculum Model. We brought in speakers from around the country to talk about national issues regarding academics, careers, work-based learning, and technology. This was a very exciting time for my colleagues and me. We felt very strongly about these changes in education, and our research encouraged us. Some of the bigger names of our presenters were Bill Daggett, who was the director of vocational education in the State of New York, Robert Glover from the US office of work-based learning (Washington), and Dr. Pat Nellor Wickwire from Hermosa, California, representing the national career-development activity at the time. We had staff from the Texas core-curriculum group visit with us, and they put on several academic workshops, including the applied-math and principles-in-technology series.

These activities began to shape and slowly influence the local educators. As each of us pressed on with our specific areas of expertise, it became evident that we were growing more knowledgeable as well. We began to deliver a lot of this information not just to local districts, but to districts throughout Michigan. I became president of the Michigan Career Placement Association and delivered several presentations throughout Michigan on the topics of placement development and high school apprenticeship systems. As our office embarked with the Apprenticeship-Development Program, we continued to organize and structure our work as efficiently as possible for all areas of career development and placement for students. We saw the students as our direct customers and the employers as our indirect customers, and we wanted both to succeed in this system. For us, success was the bottom line.

When we started the activities, we told both parents and students that we could not guarantee that their son or daughter would be placed in a certified apprenticeship program, but that it was our goal to place them all with an employer that would continue their education beyond the high school level. The technical program that most of the students participated in while in high school was for a period of two years. We had both high school juniors and seniors participating in part-time employment. During this time, we would work with them to solidify their academics, maturity, and interviewing skills. By the end of their senior year, we felt that these students would be better prepared than students that had not gone through this type of training. We also felt that it would produce top-notch students for our local employers. We knew from our process that these students would have the academics, technical skills from their prospective programs, and maturity to solidify a job once they started.

When we started this program, we had approximately thirty-five students in the first year, and most of them were high school seniors. At the end of our first year, we placed all but three of these students in jobs that had certified apprenticeship programs. Anytime a program as extensive as this one was launched, we knew it would take a period before we could get results and feedback from our customers. I must point out that the first year had more seniors in the group because it was our goal to get them prepared as fast as possible, and we knew that we would not have two years to work with them. So, they were put on a fast track, and we ran them through the program faster than we really wanted to. In doing so, we were able to streamline some of the processes we were using.

As the program continued, our student numbers rose dramatically, and in our peak year, we had approximately 170 students that were connected to a viable apprenticeship program. It may sound like a small number for a technical center that had roughly twelve hundred students attending, but only approximately one-third of the programs had certified apprenticeships associated with their individual programs. As time went on, the employers became more and more excited about this program because of the quality of the students that we were giving them. We also did an exit survey with students to ask them about their experiences with the apprenticeship program and the process that we put them through. The response was overwhelmingly positive regarding how much they felt this process helped prepare them, and they recommended it for all students, not just students who were looking at an apprenticeship program.

It was this system that got us as close as we could get to the perfect educational dual-track system. Our educational unit was in concert with business and industry trying to produce the most prepared individuals for the world of work, specifically the high-tech world of manufacturing and construction. In the last two decades, educators have fallen away or lost sight of the target, slowly moving away from CTE while keeping a narrow focus on a four-year-college track for students.

CHAPTER SEVEN

The Apprenticeship-Development Program

Looking back during the years that I worked as a career-placement coordinator with the apprenticeship system, I researched methods to connect students to employers in ways that were consistent and ongoing. It was the employers and employee unions who had control of the apprenticeship system, and it became quite clear that I needed to learn every aspect of this system to help both the student and the employer.

At first, students were recommended to several employers based on the recommendation from their instructor. These placements worked out satisfactorily for numerous students and employers. However, for some it was unsuccessful. Once a student received a referral from my office, the employer would interview them and hire them depending on the interview. I soon discovered that some students did not have the basic math, reading, or measurement skills that were needed to succeed. Numerous students also lacked maturity in handling a job and would be let go based on some of the criteria listed above. Because of the hiring and attrition rates we were experiencing, I felt it was time to address these issues. It became apparent that we needed to test students both on basic academics and where they stood in their maturity level. I developed and implemented the Apprenticeship-Development Program for high school sophomores, juniors, and seniors. This program started out with a general application of interest beginning in their sophomore year.

Mission statement for the Apprenticeship-Development Program:

Through a series of events, activities, and assessments, students will demonstrate a proficient level of academics, employability skills, and maturity to successfully enter the workforce.

The rationale for establishing the Apprenticeship-Development Program is as follows: 1) site certification, 2) academic inefficiencies, 3) number of students not completing an apprenticeship program, 4) maturity at beginning of program, 5) employability-skills issues (i.e., attendance, presentation, and work habits).

The purpose of the Apprenticeship-Development Program is to: 1) increase self-awareness of the necessary skills needed to succeed within the apprenticeship-training system, 2) solidify the necessary academic skills to succeed in the apprenticeship system, and 3) to develop the maturity to get and maintain a high-tech job within a specific area of training.

The process for achieving these outcomes was established by students interacting in a step-by-step system of measurement, reading and math assessments, academic workshops, workplace-success assessments, and employability workshops that address trainability issues, problem-solving activities such as reading charts and graphs, structured work groups, team building, communications, and portfolio workshops. This set of structured activities had a profound impact on the success of our students. Because the success rate of our students had risen so quickly after the first year, an exit survey was done with each student. Overwhelmingly, students said that they felt more prepared and confident when going into their final interview and would recommend that all students go through this process before graduation.

Initially, in the beginning, as with any new program, we wanted it to be accepted and backed by our community as well as our staff. We decided to have an orientation meeting with the parents of students who were interested in proceeding with this program. It was for students who wanted to pursue their careers in one of the many technical fields that had established apprenticeships. A flyer was sent home to the entire student body of the CTE center to inform them of the upcoming orientation. We asked that students bring a parent to attend. We wanted the support of parents behind these students because, as data has shown, when parents support the student, the success rate increases exponentially. Once the date was set for the orientation, we then proceeded with the process.

The following is the list of events held within the Apprenticeship-Development Program, beginning with the orientation and ending with the certificate of completion. Each part of the process and its purpose is described.

ORIENTATION:

The orientation was a time that we could thoroughly explain our mission and purpose to help the student become more successful and try to rally the support of the parents. We provided a local video of other students that had completed the process, and it provided a glimpse into what was set before the new students within this unique system. After the video, we had our local BAT rep speak to the parents and students about their role and what they could expect. After the BAT rep spoke, we then had the community college apprenticeship coordinator talk to the students about the related training portion of their individual programs.

It was at this time that we opened it up for questions with the parents and students regarding the Apprenticeship-Development Program. This usually lasted about fifteen minutes. Before we adjourned, I gave the students their first assignment, which was to talk it over with their parents, decide, and then turn in their application.

APPLICATION:

The application was the beginning of the process for the students. This was when the responsibility shifted to the student. For the student to be accepted into the apprenticeship program, they needed to fill out the application and return it to the work-based learning office by a specific date and signed by one of their parents. No exceptions were allowed. If an application came in late, these students would be placed in a pool for the following year.

INTERVIEW:

Once the application was turned into the work-based learning office, an interview date was set up with one of the career-placement coordinators. At this interview, students were asked about their careers and their commitment to their goals regarding any future technical training and job placement. We evaluated how much each student was committed to following their current career path and if they were matched properly with their career training. We explained that the program process was designed to measure their commitment to their specific career, measure their academic skills, and assess their maturity levels at the beginning and the end of this process. From the interview, the student received a profile on their readiness for both the academic and maturity level. With this profile, students were categorized for placement in upcoming workshops based on their individual needs.

ACADEMIC ASSESSMENTS/ACADEMIC WORKSHOPS:

One of the first workshops set up for students was academic assessments. Even though students may have had a fair to good grade point average in their academic area, we administered this assessment to all of them. We used a nationally normed test to give us an accurate view of their math, reading, and measurement skills. Once the students completed this assessment and scored over 90 percent, they were excused from any additional math, reading, or measurement workshops. All academic workshops were taught by certified teachers with expertise in math, English, and measurement skills.

EMPLOYABILITY-SKILLS ASSESSMENTS:

The fourth item in our process for students was the employability assessment. One of the assessments we chose for this step was the

"Workplace-Success Assessment." This assessment is also nationally normed and gets at the readiness of employees for working in the workplace and helps us assess problem-solving skills as they relate to the workplace environment. Students view actual work-environment situations and answer questions based on their current knowledge. This assessment also helps us evaluate the student's maturity level early in the process, which assists us in providing additional workshops to help them grow in this area. Therefore, we start them in their sophomore or junior year. This gives us approximately 1.5–2 years to help the student prepare for their final job interview.

EMPLOYABILITY WORKSHOPS:

Many of the employability workshops were given by the coordinators in our placement office. Some workshops featured current employees who discussed how to act in the workplace and what is expected from some of our local employers. One of the workshops that was most effective was a workshop put on by the Future of Work Group. This workshop covered everything from attendance to taking notes, employee relations and quality control issues. Many of these workshops were mandatory workshops for all apprenticeship-program students. Because these workshops were so good and powerful, we even invited some of the senior students who had not applied for the apprenticeship program.

PORTFOLIO WORKSHOPS:

After students had moved through most of the workshops and were progressing along in good standing, we then scheduled them for one of their final events, called the portfolio workshop. These workshops were given to students by the coordinators, who would explain what a portfolio was and how it could be used in their final interview. At this point in the process, students would begin on their portfolio and continue updating it until their departure from the technical center program. As students were going through many of the workshops, they were expected to complete several job shadows with employers and, if possible, participate in an internship with an employer. All this activity would lead up to one of the final events in the process, and that was the mock interviews.

MOCK INTERVIEWS:

Each year we brought in several business and industry personnel, most of whom were HR people and were experienced with interviewing job candidates. These mock interviews were designed to give students practice in interviewing and receive direct feedback on things that were good to talk about, and things that were not. I cannot stress enough the importance of these interviews to the process. Usually, employers would be fairly impressed with the preparedness of the students, but if any glitches occurred, students would get direct feedback and the opportunity to correct it before the real interviews occurred. For many of the apprenticeship-program students, this process took just under two years, but for a few seniors that would have a career change and were quite serious about their future, they would be allowed in the program but expected to complete all the necessary workshops before their senior year ended.

CERTIFICATE OF COMPLETION:

Students completing all the required assessments and workshops were given a certificate of completion for the Apprenticeship-Development Program, and then they were set up with interviews for their given area and sent out to employers. Remarkably, we had a very high success rate for the participating students. Employers were elated with the students that we were providing, and some employers did not want to see any other students except for the students who completed this process. I am not saying to you that this is the only process that would work at this level, but it did prove to be highly successful in preparing students for many of the technical jobs at that time.

The Importance of the Apprenticeship-Development Program

One of the problems associated with our educational system is the attitude that all students need to attend a four-year college. I do agree that students may need some postsecondary education, but not necessarily a four-year degree. Many of the apprenticeship students receive two years of related postsecondary training (classes) in their technical area, such as electronics, HVAC, or carpentry, all of which require a high level of math skills to be successful. Many of these students do finish an associate's degree, and after gaining confidence, some even go on for a four-year degree or even a master's degree as I did. Our current educational system is not designed for the hands-on type of learner, but rather is designed for the academic learner. This is one of the main reasons that I feel our educational system needs changes, and we must develop the technical track and put it running parallel to the academic track as a dual, split, or Y-track system.

I believe this program was instrumental in placing a very high percentage of available students from our CTE center into jobs during a fifteen-year period. The upgrading and processing of these students was the closest one can get to a seamless Y-track system.

This is where we need to be now in America. With a Y-track system, the nearly half of students who do not attend college to completion will no longer be discriminated against, and they'll be able to pursue a fulfilling career path. This will keep our middle class very strong and will bolster our manufacturing base, along with balancing our entire economy. We must recognize the talents of our people and develop a technical track parallel to our academic track. I developed this process in the mid-nineties, and it has proven to be an extremely effective preparational process for young high school students and adults.

CHAPTER EIGHT

Introduction to the American Apprenticeship System

It was during the fall of 1990 that I began to research the European and German models of education. In the German model, preschool and elementary education resemble the US in the fact that all their students are combined in a school called Grundschule, known in the US as elementary school. All students remain in Grundschule from four to six years, like our first through sixth grade here in America. After testing, students are recommended by their teachers to pursue one of three tracks, the Hauptschule (lowest track), Realschule (middle track), or the Gymnasium (college track). The first few years of these tracks are the orientation years and considered to be general in nature with emphasis on teaching reading, writing, and mathematics. Each track has some vocational training, and they are funded by their local, district, and federal government.

The Hauptschule is the track that most resembles our form of apprenticeship, but it occurs much earlier than in our educational delivery. Strong local training and support are areas where the American system is like the German system, and this practice of supplying locally skilled workers to local companies allows for the needed product and moving their human resources through with a steady flow both at the business level and the academic level. It achieves maximizing their human resources to the highest level and helps their business partners become more competitive in the global market.

Germany's three-track system holds students accountable and

allows them purpose and direction for their future. In many of our cities, young people without guidance for a viable career path are looking for purpose and a sense of belonging. There are many students that flounder in the US system and waste a great amount of time doing so. Many students struggle while searching for what they're passionate about or what they would like to do. This is why career education needs to be plugged into the system throughout the K–12 educational plan.

In examining both the European and American systems, I found that a few items are much the same regarding the early years of education, but significant differences arise at approximately age fourteen. At this time, European students decide whether they'd like to pursue either a college track or a more technical track associated with apprenticeship training. It is this split where students take different paths to their prospective careers, and this is what is called a "dual-track" system. This is similar to how the US operates CTE. However, we don't place as much emphasis on apprenticeships and certainly do not help direct our students into a focused career path. The European model's biggest drawback is the fact that once a student begins on one of the tracks, it does not allow much flexibility to change or cross over to another track due to testing assessments. Though their system seems to be evolving and growing more flexible over time, the American model has historically allowed for better movement if a student changes his or her mind. In the US, many people start a specific career and then switch to something new, going back to receive additional training in their newly chosen field. I did this myself. Being trained as a carpenter first, I decided to go to college and continue paying for my education through my trade. When this occurs, a three-to-five-year period of low productivity takes place, and the student loses time and money. This is very typical for our American students, as many are pushed on to college with the expectation of financial stability—but it doesn't always work out that way.

Employers need a highly skilled and prepared workforce to take them to entry level and beyond training. Career centers are some of the most critical areas in the US for the delivery of high-tech human resources. Approximately 1,300,000 students were enrolled in vocational-education programs in Germany as of 2017. In the US, only 190,000 students were registered for apprenticeship programs in the same year.[20] European nations prioritize vocational training for many students, with half of secondary students participating in vocational programs. In the US, since the passage of the 1944 GI Bill, the college-bound path has been pushed over vocational education. This "college-for-all" narrative has been emphasized for decades as the pathway to success and stability.[21]

Our system in the US was formally operated through a federal branch of the Department of Labor, the Bureau of Apprenticeship and Training (BAT). Most of the day-to-day operations were delivered by our local companies, who shouldered most of the cost for the US system by opening training sites. After studying and comparing the German, European, and American systems, I believe the US could put together a much more efficient type of educational delivery that would serve our society and our business community, at the same time utilizing public taxes and human resources more efficiently.

My original knowledge of apprenticeships was based on the personal experience of being an apprentice at an early age and teaching carpentry apprentices for nine years at a community college. When I started in my role as a work-based learning coordinator, I began contacting various groups involved in apprenticeships and soon discovered that I needed to learn a great deal more about the apprenticeship system. In addition to working with K–12 school counselors, I needed more insight from the perspective of business owners, human resources staff, community college coordinators,

---

20   Ann-Cathrin Spees, "Could Germany's Vocational Education and Training System Be a Model for the U.S.?" World Education News + Reviews, June 12, 2018, https://wenr.wes.org/2018/06/could-germanys-vocational-education-and-training-system-be-a-model-for-the-u-s.

21   St-Esprit, "The Stigma of Choosing Trade School Over College."

and the BAT staff. In the beginning, 1990, we called it the Early Apprenticeship Program, and later, in approximately 1992, it was renamed the School-to-Registered Apprenticeship Program.

I began communicating with many employers in our local area that were operating apprenticeship programs. It took some time to get useful information from employers because businesses do not like to divulge much information about their training. I discovered that some companies were spending a lot of money training apprentices and then a company down the road would offer the apprentice more money after their training was completed, effectively "stealing" them away. The company stealing the employee had no investment in their training, so they felt they could offer more pay to the apprentice and get that much further ahead. This became a contentious problem for several companies, and it's exactly why we need a universal buy-in across our country.

As I began working more in-depth with apprenticeships, I got to know the players and personnel that managed the day-to-day operations of the apprenticeship system. When collaborating with a company with a joint apprenticeship committee, I needed to call in the BAT representative. We were cutting new ground regarding student-wage and hour issues, and they wanted a government representative on-site. There were different requirements for a joint apprenticeship committee. The apprenticeship system had many parts, and there was not a good "how to" book or format for employers and schools to easily put these fragmented pieces together. At that time, I put together a handbook called the "School-to-Registered Apprenticeship Handbook." This was done to help students and parents understand the process and how our students would proceed through this apprenticeship system.

Another facet that I learned about the system was in related training. I spent a good share of time, six to seven years, working with the community college staff in shaping and updating much of the related training curricula. I was trying to stop some of the duplication that was occurring between the secondary technical center and the local community college. This updating of the apprenticeship curricula was one reason the state recognized the STRA program and then awarded the STRA apprentice one thousand hours of on-the-job (OTC) credit when they completed the high school portion of their apprenticeship. This helped the employer get the apprentice to journeyman status faster and accelerated their pay level. If we started a new apprenticeship that had no formal related training at the community college, then we delivered the training at the technical center in an adult program in one of the evening classes.

My personal "apprenticeship" experience began when I was twelve years old. I was basically forced into working for my father's building-construction business. I had progressed into a downward spiral by "feeling my oats," sneaking out at night and getting into trouble with a couple of friends. When my father found out, he warned me about being responsible for my actions. I had two older brothers and was accustomed to fighting things out with them. Then, I started to have more trouble at school with a few fights and was also caught cheating on an exam. Once my parents were called to school, I knew I was in big trouble.

My father handled it very calmly but sternly by taking me for a visit to a boys' reform school just to the north of where we lived. He brought me up to the fence that surrounded the school and said, "If you have one more incident in school, this is where you are going." My father was a WWII Marine veteran who had been shot through the hip and survived. I knew he meant business, and these were not idle words. He had experienced the good and bad of this world and wanted only the best for me. The next Saturday he got me out of bed to the delight of my older brothers, and he took me to work with him. That summer he had me ride to jobs with him so he could keep an eye on me, and I began working for his business. My jobs included digging trenches for electrical and sewer lines, installing dry wells, hooking up dry well plumbing, and tarring basements for every new house his company built. I wasn't very happy about this at first, but eventually it changed my life focus. I worked every day during the summer and frequently on Saturdays. Although it wasn't a classroom, my father taught me about hard work and a sense of accomplishment. To my delight, I also earned money.

When I was fourteen, I asked my father if I could move to the framing crew. He approved, and I learned how to frame a house, put up siding, install windows and doors, and shingle roofs. This was before builders had SkyTraks and had to carry the lumber and shingles to the roof by our own strength. My dad's business had numerous foremen, and at first they looked at me as a young undisciplined kid. When I started on the framing crew, after proving how hard I could work by digging ditches and the like, they were very welcoming. Two of the framing foremen took me under their wing and taught me all the tricks of the trade, including a lot of math problems that dealt with calculations for laying out rafters and cutting stair stringers for steps. One of my mentors was six foot six and could reach the ceilings without a ladder. I soaked up all the knowledge like a sponge, and they were always willing to explain and show me new ways to do certain procedures. When I was sixteen, I was moved to the finishing crew. This is where I learned how to build stairways, hang kitchen cabinets, install trim, paint, and stain. I also worked on exterior painting/staining and trim, and I learned how to proceed with many procedural steps regarding prepping plastered walls as well as drywall for painting residential homes. Between sixteen and eighteen, I began doing side remodeling jobs with one of the foremen on Saturdays.

During the summer between high school graduation and college, my father asked me if I would like to try to build a "spec" house from start to finish. I was very excited about this prospect and said I would love to. I handled all the paperwork, hired the subs, did the scheduling, and more. It was a very successful experience and gave me a lot of confidence. When I went to college at age nineteen, I was able to pay for my tuition and living expenses by doing remodeling, additions, new kitchens, finished basements, and other jobs. When word got out to the professors about my skills, I did a lot of carpentry work for them throughout my stay at the university.

I mention my background to show that when young people are left without direction and purpose, trouble shows up. I was very fortunate to have a strong father as my teacher and mentor. Things were quickly going downhill for me, and if he had not stepped up to the plate to straighten me out, I could have easily become a teenage street thug. For the students who are getting little to no input and support from their family or no directional goals from their educational system, walking out of high school for the last time can bring a very empty feeling. Without family support, a mentor, school counselors, or career education, once students reach the end of high school, it becomes harder to seek out a successful career. This is why I believe the German system is ahead of the US, because their students are engaged in a system with clear expectations—a job—very early on.

However, Americans are becoming more enlightened about our shortage of skilled workers and the additional training that must take place to solve the problem. In Michigan, the governor recently approved free community college tuition for CTE classes associated with the apprenticeship system. This is a very positive step in the right direction, and it balances some of the funding discrepancies. However, more funding and the exposure of different career paths to K–12 students is necessary. A Y-track system should not discriminate and must be equally supported by the people, government, and businesses alike. All the components are there. This would help remove the stigma that success is only found in a four-year-college degree. It's true: To make a respectable living, some students may need some coursework and training at the college level. This would apply in mastering the high-tech world of manufacturing, such as tool and die makers, CNC machinists, and mold makers. All these occupations require a high level of mathematics. We have a good system of training in the US now, but it is costing our employers too much to compete. And, as stated previously, some employers will not invest in the training but are happy to steal good employees away from other employers who are investing in their human resources.

The German VET (vocational education and training) system is supported by federal, local, and state funds based on population and is unified across their country. This is another reason why their youth unemployment is so low.[22] Because the US doesn't have a unified national system like this, we cannot find enough skilled workers to fill all of the job openings. Many of these jobs would fit into our apprenticeship system. For this reason alone, we need to become more unified across our country and establish a national balance across our educational system. The educational institutions need to recognize CTE and vocational education as a viable route to success, and it needs to be funded equally. This will help all sectors of our economy to flourish and grow.

The first step in developing a Y-track system is to expose this issue in the working world as well as our higher-education institutions. Since I began authoring this book fifteen years ago, not much has happened in CTE around the country. Today, there are several initiatives that have been spawned, for example, "The Skills Initiative: Expanding Apprenticeship in the U.S.—Lessons from the German Dual Education System."[23]

Today, many German companies have started initiatives that are engaging with local industry in several US states. To begin establishing a national framework, we should implement a national School-to-Registered Apprenticeship system and ensure each school has access to

---

22 Ann-Cathrin Spees, "Could Germany's Vocational Education and Training System Be a Model for the U.S.?"

23 Embassy of the Federal Republic of Germany, "The Skills Initiative: Expanding Apprenticeship in the U.S.—Lessons from the German Dual Education System," effective May 2025, https://www.germany.info/resource/blob/649542/35e0d1e2c95155704105b9013dd279bb/skills-whitepaper-data.pdf.

many of the CTE courses currently in place at the secondary technical centers. This would save America a lot of wasted money and human resources.

The expansion of vocational and technical education will need to be done on a national level. It could also be implemented on a trial basis regionally, especially in "rust belt" states, which have a high percentage of apprenticeships traditionally. Michigan, Ohio, Wisconsin, and Pennsylvania would also be good locations to implement an expansion in vocational training and CTE. I personally prefer developing this system nationally, to get America back on track with reducing our dependence on foreign companies.

At the technical center where I was employed for fifteen years, our process was working very well, but it wasn't a solidified, permanent system. Some of the components remain with the BAT. Statewide, we were getting recognition for what we were doing, but once money became tight and a few of us retired, all efforts ceased. I see and hear many people talking about our problems, but we keep sliding farther away from great solutions that are proven to be successful, and I feel a responsibility to get this out into the public domain. This is one of the keys to rebuilding the American middle class and stopping the discrimination against students that do not fit into the college-track box. Without this type of system, we cannot have a highly trained and educated workforce.

The American Apprenticeship System

The American Apprenticeship System seems like it should be easy to understand. However, whether you are an employer, placement coordinator, or human-resource director, working with the apprenticeship system can be confusing or even baffling at times. This confusion can arise because the people working within the system do not understand the roles of their counterparts, and as a result they don't understand the framework as a whole. Part of the problem lies in the fact that there is a lack of formal training and resources available that explain how to incorporate CTE and apprenticeships throughout the K–12 educational system effectively.

The rationale for writing this book is to lay out the pathway to help people pull this system together and integrate it into a split, dual, or Y-track educational system that engages students in apprenticeships while they are still in high school. Because there are so many involved players in the apprenticeship system, things can become overwhelming and cloudy. People need to first understand who manages and pays for the system so they can effectively navigate it with the proper support. In the following paragraphs, I will explain the major entities and players that are and may be involved in the system.

If the sponsor (employer) is working with an internal cosponsor, such as a union or secondary school, then the number of players will increase. The US apprenticeship system is fragmented between three different entities, including the employer, the BAT representative (Bureau of Apprenticeship and Training), the college apprenticeship coordinator, and the STRA coordinator (School-to-Registered Apprenticeship) or high school coordinator. In our educational system and in a Y-track system, these would be the main representatives that would be a part of walking an apprentice through the system from start to finish.

At the end of their training, apprenticeship completers would receive a four-year apprenticeship certificate in a specific technical area and, for many, have completed two years of postsecondary education, leading to an associate's degree from their local community college. These individuals are then qualified to go into high-paying skilled jobs or will have the confidence to go on to college if they choose.

The main player in the apprenticeship system is the apprentice. An apprentice may be a male or female and must be at least fourteen years of age. Students can begin apprenticeships during the high school level, college level, or beyond. The apprentice must have an adequate foundation in academic subjects to include reading, measurement, and mathematics. In addition, depending on the job description, the apprentice must have an aptitude for the basic skills required for the job. He or she must possess the physical capability and maturity level to function in a professional setting.

The employer is the most significant player in the apprenticeship system. Employers are rarely given the credit they deserve for their dedication and work regarding the training of many Americans. They should be applauded for their role. The employer (and the union if one exists) is basically responsible for funding an apprenticeship. The employer is referred to as the "sponsor," and without a sponsor, there is no job or training site for employees and students. Usually, if the sponsor is a large business or company, then it is likely there will be a union involved. I have worked with smaller companies with apprenticeship programs in place but do not have union involvement. With a small-business type of format, fewer people are involved as cosponsors, which can speed up the process for the apprentice. If a union is present, there normally is a joint apprenticeship committee composed of union folks and people from management. These committees usually manage the day-to-day paperwork along with the company's HR people in registering the apprentice with the BAT.

The union, also known as the cosponsor, is also a key player, and I really need to give some accolades to these organizations, because in the beginning of their existence this was their focus and function. The efforts of the unions have improved working conditions and wages, and they are responsible for much of the training for America's workforce in many of the technical areas. This is a critical foundation of America's middle class. It is the middle class that has driven prosperity in America for the last seventy years. The unions worked to provide certified training for all employees that were capable of learning the information required to become a journey person in one of the many certified training programs that have developed in the US. Unions should be publicly explaining to citizens what they have accomplished and what they have done for our overall society in general. Unfortunately, some union leaders have lost focus of their true function, which is to provide workers with technical training, improve the work environment, and help the company become more successful. These unions have been overly concentrated on their political involvement.

The third player is the educational institution or related training facility. Throughout America the landscape has been fostered or enhanced by our local community colleges. Community colleges, because of their proximity to local business, became natural deliverers of the needed related training for employees, fulfilling the requirements of both the BAT and employer. Every apprenticeship program has 576 hours of related training attached to it out of the eight thousand hours that are required for most certified training programs. Over seven thousand hours are on-the-job training, normally with a journey person until the apprentice is fully trained.

Once an apprentice completes their related training, it puts them very close to an associate's degree. Many students will pick up some of the needed social studies and English requirements to complete their degree. An apprentice will take one class each semester for four years, and each class is worth approximately seventy-two hours of related training hours and recognized by higher education in almost all cases throughout the US. Eight classes over four years will give the employee the 576 hours that are needed to complete their prospective program. Most often these classes are layered with math and science knowledge and can be very technical. In most cases they will follow some of the pre-engineering classes. I taught these classes for nine years at a community college for the construction trades, and I also worked on some of the new programs and helped coordinate new classes that were being developed between the CTE centers and community colleges. This stopped duplication from secondary education to postsecondary education and also allowed the student or employee to speed up their training and complete it early, beneficial both to the employee and the employer.

The fourth player in this unique system is the BAT. This branch of the Department of Labor was put in place under the Davis–Bacon Act of 1937 and is the agency that manages the American apprenticeship system. They're the group that approves and denies the certifications, and they're also the agency that provides the certificates of completion based on the employer's recommendations. This agency also provides the set of standards that each skill or sponsor is governed by. Each set of standards represents or contains the same twenty-four standards that represent the terminology, rules, and regulations that govern all apprenticeship programs registered under the US Department of Labor.[24]

With the involvement of secondary technical schools, there can be one more player, and that's the school-to-apprenticeship coordinator that represents the secondary technical school. This person is responsible for locating and prepping a student while in high school. In the beginning, this program was called the Early Apprenticeship Program and later became known as the "School-to-Registered Apprenticeship Program" for Michigan. The coordinator was referred to as the STRA coordinator

---

24 For more information regarding standards, please visit the following website address: https://www.apprenticeship.gov/sites/default/files/apprenticeship-requirements-reference-guide.pdf.

CHAPTER NINE

In Conclusion: Implementing the Y-Track System of Education

Higher education has long dictated our K–12 educational system, pushing more and more people to go to college. Today our system is failing, simply because we are producing more students geared toward a college education, especially in the liberal-arts area. Many of these liberal-arts graduates have difficulty finding jobs in their career specialty. As referenced in chapter 1, research has shown that 62 percent of students go on to college, and 36 percent of that group eventually drops out.[25] Because of the previous trade deals, higher governmental taxes, and numerous regulations, many of our manufacturing jobs have gone to foreign countries such as China. At the same time, many of the technical educational areas have been cut back, leaving a void or gap in the supply of technically trained people. Early in the industrial revolution and as late as the 1970s, students could graduate from high school and go to work for an industrial-based manufacturer, work for thirty years, earn a pension, and retire.

Today, however, we are in an information, technology, and services society, and people are changing jobs two to four times in their careers. Hence, people have been pushed to go on to college and get a degree that will allow them to achieve a thirty-year career with some stability. Poised by this thinking and the need to pursue higher

---

25 National Center for Education Statistics, "Undergraduate Retention and Graduation Rates."

education, many schools and their counselors push hard to drive students away from the technical and skilled areas. Unfortunately, in many high schools, students are pushed on to college and, after giving it a go for a short time, find themselves dropping out and picking up part-time and some full-time jobs that do not require much schooling and are paid accordingly. After trudging through college for a few years, many of these hands-on, technically minded individuals find themselves working with an employer in an apprenticeship program toward a journeyman card or certificate, whether associated with a union or not. These individuals are then on a solid path to a solid career with good wages and salaries.

In education, change—or the idea of change—is always in the wind. I remember many of my colleagues and fellow educators complaining about the newest wave sweeping across the country that would finally "fix" education. For many educators who had been around for a long while, it would be just another trend that may or may not help. I always looked at the newest idea for an educational remedy with a slanted eye and hoped it had something that I could use or improve my teaching with. I often felt that many of the good educators would spin these new improvement ideas positively and internalize it, even though they did not have much to offer. For many educators, the latest spin is not the solution, but rather a PR spin to give the outside world the thought that something is being done to education that will make it better. Given this information, I always felt that I could get something to take away from the latest workshops that would assist or reinforce what I was currently doing as an educator.

I spoke briefly in chapter 2 about improving education, and if the US is serious about doing that, then a concentrated effort will need to take place in building, supporting, and maintaining healthy families. The family structure is the fundamental key in making our schools successful. Strengthening the family support system can be accomplished by numerous methods. First, we should implement tax incentives or reduce taxes for the family based on the number of children they have. We must try to set up more incentives and support for families and make it a national goal to promote family life. If the family structure crumbles, so will the schools and our country. I gave examples in the earlier chapters about three steps for improving education. One, we should put a larger number of resources toward the preschool years for reading programs and assistance for parents who cannot read. Two, we should develop a technical track equal to the academic track. Three, we should implement a K–12 Y-track career-development delivery for all students in our educational systems, both private and public.

To make changes in policy and structure, the right people and resources need to be brought together. Change would require a temporary board with the right people that come from all areas of our workforce and communities. The research is there, but it always gets fragmented by small groups throughout the country. In many cases these groups mean well but do not have the resources to implement their ideas on a grand scale, and many of these great initiatives just fizzle out. I refer to our initiative through the Applied-Technology Curriculum Model. We put millions of dollars behind this initiative as well as a good-sized staff, and we began to see a significant change in the local school districts and how education was delivered. As soon as we stopped putting resources and personnel behind this initiative, the system slowly returned to its original state, or what had been in place before the Applied-Technology Curriculum Model was implemented.

Our initiative impacted approximately fifteen years of significant changes. But very few original innovators remained, and therefore putting the right people in place will make the difference. Education needs leadership on a grand scale, and when you look around, there are some good leaders, but many do not want to step up and take the chance of failing or spearhead a large initiative. If the right number of resources don't follow through, then it may end up as a short-term job. With this up-and-down tide occurring in education, it becomes harder and harder to make real change. A similar rationale can be made when one examines how our CTE is delivered.

Because of the way that the apprenticeship system is designed, the system receives very little attention. Many of the state and national unions cosponsor apprenticeships and are funding much of the training along with employers. Companies that have joint apprenticeship committees share these training fees with management. This information is not being discussed nationally today. Basically, because very few people understand or even know how our system is being delivered, many times the unions are bashed regarding what they do and their purpose. I believe all the politicians who support right-to-work state legislation need to take into consideration that very few apprenticeships exist today without union support. The question is, "Do you want to get good technical training as part of your employment, or do you want to go to work for a company that provides very little training and, therefore, can pay you less and make larger profits, leaving you with little or no mobility after a small amount of training?" As a consumer, I would rather pay slightly more for a vehicle that is made in America knowing that it is constructed to the highest standards and the employees will be able to live comfortably in the middle class as a family, as opposed to buying a foreign car and watching the profits benefit a foreign country. In addition, companies are now finding out that with our technology and a well-trained workforce, we can outperform other countries that have cheaper labor.

To implement a Y-track system that is integrated with the apprenticeship system will take many of the right-minded people and a national focus with top-notch leadership. First and foremost, the country would have to agree across the board that to improve our educational system, a Y-track system focused on technical skills and apprenticeships needs to be elevated as an equal system alongside our academic college-bound track. This would help improve the development of our human resources in the US. We need to balance the funding, lower the cost for a college education, and establish

CTE as a parallel path to our academic education. Second, a state-by-state committee would need to be formed, similar to the state committees I served on in Michigan that wrote some of the school-to-work grants and work-based learning grants. These were nonpartisan groups of people who were experts in their given areas and brought together specifically to write a grant to help Michigan youth make the transition from school to work. This youth included students that were heading into postsecondary tech prep or higher education and then into a job. Everyone needs to realize that all education should serve one common outcome: securing a job. Unfortunately, many of the educational endeavors today do not match up with the specific demands for a trained workforce or current trends. This translates into billions of dollars and substantial time wasted, as well as years of misdirecting our human resources. America cannot continue to waste time and money on the education of our young people and expect to continue being a world leader.

In the Y-track system, once students are in our educational system and getting closer to their freshman experience, they would take a series of career- and personal-interest assessments to help them in their decision to choose a path. Once students have made their decision, they would be directed through a walkthrough of their prospective career. With assistance from a career counselor, students would explore the classes they will have while still in high school and if any postsecondary classes or additional training is needed for the technical skill area they may pursue. A walkthrough would end with the job that the prospective path may lead to.

For example, Student A might take a path which requires a four-year-college degree beyond high school and graduates as an engineer with a full-time job while Student B walks through their prospective path during high school and is placed in a part-time job with an employer as an apprentice. This student will go through one of the technical schools that already exists in our system and then go on after high school to a local community college and complete his or her related training to finish a journeyman's certificate as a tool and die maker. Both paths would share in the American school fund that would be set up locally and monitored by local boards. In Michigan, these could be overseen by the regional ISDs. This system would save America billions of dollars in educational funds and increase the development of our human resources, as well as save our employers on training costs, which would make them more competitive globally.

A national oversight committee would need to be assembled to keep good ideas from one state to another flowing back and forth. The national oversight committee would be made up of the head of the Department of Education, head of the Bureau of Apprenticeship and Training or Office of Work-Based Learning, and six CEOs from the business and industry sector. The six CEOs should have different backgrounds, such as two from manufacturing, two from any of the construction trades, two from the medical field, and two from the computer-tech areas. Also, the oversight committee should have two people from placement agencies, three people representing national union labor, several members that are affiliated with joint apprenticeship committees, and several smaller union-shop members Also, representing labor should be AGC (Associated General Contractors) and ABC (Associated Builders and Contractors). One to represent the union workers, and one to represent the nonunion workforce in construction. In addition, this board must have a group of parents from several different communities that represent the city areas as well as the rural areas, and the committee would need to meet at least once a month. These assignments could be paid or unpaid and would only stay in place until the system was up and running smoothly. An implementation board would need to work in the local areas. In Michigan, districts are managed by local or regional ISDs, and these ISDs could implement the Y-track system. Along with school-improvement staff from the ISD, a crew of coordinators will need to be set in place to assist the transition from high school to postsecondary training sites and worksites for those who will be using the apprenticeship track. For many, this proposed Y-track idea may seem like an enormous task, but it is merely connecting many of the existing components of our educational system in a more organized and structured manner. We had this system working in the 1990s, and then when money got tight and some of the placement staff was let go or retired, our ISD decided to shut the program down. This was the only program that connected young people with real jobs and postsecondary related training. It was a sad day for our placement staff and for future students as well. This is why leadership matters!

Conclusion

I'm proposing a new system in which, beginning in kindergarten, students are exposed to speakers from a wide variety of businesses and industries. This career program should run through the ninth grade. After the ninth grade and a series of career assessments, students would decide which track of education they would like to pursue, a track to a four-year college education and degree, or a more technical track leading to additional college or a four-year apprenticeship certificate. These two separate tracks would begin in the tenth grade, and students in both tracks would plan to continue education after high school. While some students would proceed to a four-year college, the other students would begin their related training classes at the community college while continuing their specific hands-on training at the employer they started with in high school. For this new system, the biggest changes would take place in grades ten through twelve. Overall, instead of just neglecting students who don't plan to go to college, we'd instead be putting them on track for a technical career.

This method is called the Y-track system because during the early years of all students' education, the only thing that changes is the addition of career exploration and assessments along their growing journey. The interaction with business and industry along with skilled people will help them understand that the overall goal for "growing up" is to contribute to society and prosper individually by doing a job that serves our world—and this goal can be met through countless different paths.

This revitalized approach would streamline our educational system and develop our human resources to their full potential in much less time. By having an equally funded Y-track system in place, we can build the middle class, shorten the development time of our human resources, and help our young people thrive without discriminating against one-half of our student body.

BIBLIOGRAPHY

Adhikari, Arthak, and Tamara Mickle. "What Is the Unemployed People Per Job Openings Ratio? A 21-Year Case Study into Unemployment Trends." *Beyond the Numbers* 1, no. 6 (U.S. Bureau of Labor Statistics, 2022): https://www.bls.gov/opub/btn/volume-11/what-is-the-unemployed-people-per-job-openings-ratio-a-21-year-case-study-into-unemployment-trends.htm

Apprenticeship.gov. "Did You Know?" Homepage. Effective May 2025. https://www.apprenticeship.gov/.

Embassy of the Federal Republic of Germany. "The Skills Initiative: Expanding Apprenticeship in the U.S.—Lessons from the German Dual Education System." Effective May 2025. https://www.germany.info/resource/blob/649542/35e0d1e2c95155704105b9013dd279bb/skills-whitepaper-data.pdf.

Henry, Barbara. "Highest Paying Trades." NSHSS, April 29, 2024. https://www.nshss.org/resources/blog/blog-posts/highest-paying-trades/.

Heritage, Andrew. "Skyrocketing Pharmaceutical Imports to the U.S. Endanger National Security." Coalition for a Prosperous America, January 9, 2023. https://prosperousamerica.org/skyrocketing-pharmaceutical-imports-to-the-u-s-endanger-national-security/.

Michigan Department of Education. "Annual Career Authorization." Effective May 2025. https://www.michigan.gov/mde/services/ed-serv/ed-cert/permits-placement/annual-career-authorization.

National Center for Education Statistics. "Annual Earnings by Educational Attainment." Condition of Education. Last updated May 2024. https://nces.ed.gov/programs/coe/indicator/cba.

National Center for Education Statistics. "Immediate College Enrollment Rate." Condition of Education. Last updated May 2024. https://nces.ed.gov/programs/coe/indicator/cpa.

National Center for Education Statistics. "PISA 2022 U.S. Results." https://nces.ed.gov/surveys/pisa/pisa2022/index.asp

National Center for Education Statistics. "Postsecondary Institution Revenues." Condition of Education. Last updated August 2023. https://nces.ed.gov/programs/coe/indicator/cud.

National Center for Education Statistics. "Undergraduate Retention and Graduation Rates." Condition of Education. Last updated May 2022. https://nces.ed.gov/programs/coe/indicator/ctr.

Perkins Collaborative Resource Network. "Perkins V." Legislation and Regulations. Effective May 2025. https://cte.ed.gov/legislation/perkins-v.

Spees, Ann-Catherin. "Could Germany's Vocational Education and Training System Be a Model for the U.S.?" World Education News + Reviews, June 12, 2018. https://wenr.wes.org/2018/06/could-germanys-vocational-education-and-training-system-be-a-model-for-the-u-s.

St-Esprit, Meg. "The Stigma of Choosing Trade School Over College." *The Atlantic*, March 6, 2019. https://www.theatlantic.com/education/archive/2019/03/choosing-trade-school-over-college/584275/.

United States Census Bureau. "Current Population Survey: 2022 Annual Social and Economic (ASEC) Supplement." Effective May 2025. https://www2.census.gov/programs-surveys/cps/techdocs/cpsmar22.pdf.

Wigfall, Catrin. "State Initiatives Work to Eliminate Lingering Stigma of 'Vocational' Education." American Experiment, March 22, 2018. https://www.americanexperiment.org/state-initiatives-work-to-eliminate-lingering-stigma-of-vocational-education/.

www.ingramcontent.com/pod-product-compliance
Lightning Source LLC
LaVergne TN
LVHW091545070526
838199LV00002B/217